Jessica Lorimer is a Sa motivational speaker. She is t Smart Leaders Sell Podcast a Facebook community, The Smart Leaders Sales Society. Jessica has been featured in Forbes, Huffington Post, YFS, LBC, Channel 5 and appeared on a variety of well known podcasts and summits and is well known for providing simple sales advice that help 'normal' people become great salespeople.

Learn more about Jessica at SmartLeadersSell.com

SMART LEADERS SELL

TAKING THE BS OUT OF BUSINESS

Jessica Lorimer

First Printing: 2018

ISBN 978-1-9993120-0-8

CONTENTS

CHAPTER 1: HOW THIS BOOK WILL HELP YOU ACHIEVE ALL OF YOUR SALES GOALS

**Disclaimer: I'll be honest… there are many things that I'm good at in life.

Sales. Monetising messages. Helping people to profit from their passions. Eating burritos (seriously - I won a competition and was the first woman ever in a small shop in Portsmouth, UK to attempt and eat a foot long burrito in less than an hour... #LifeGoals) But despite now being a credible author… I'm pretty grammatically challenged. I also swear like a sailor, neck tequila like a trooper and fly planes like a pilot. And only one of those is a fib. Seriously though, if you're a total grammar nut, some of my sentences in this book will not make you happy. Do me a favour though - if you spot them, email me about them by all means. But don't expect me to change the book because the print run is already out…

I also want to preface this book by saying that *holds breath* I'm NOT a Law of Attraction junkie. I'm really not 'woo'. I'm more of an action kind of girl. And so if you ARE an LOA fan, that's totally cool - and if you also love late night chats, slices of cake and belly laughing - we can still be friends. It's just that LOA isn't in my zone of genius - so when you read this book, be open minded. And remember… some of my very best friends and most respected colleagues absolutely love 'The Woo'... so I can totally jam on it with intelligent discussions over a moody espresso. Or a large glass of Prosecco if I'm honest.

Anyway, time to crack on. Only actionable, implementable pages ahead - be open minded, ignore the swearing/ grammatical/ spelling errors - and just take exactly what you need.

Grab a coffee and let's roll.

Why buy this book?

Right now, I'm writing this, imagining that you - gorgeous reader - are sat wondering exactly what this book is going to be about. I imagine that you grabbed it off the shelf because it a) promises sales strategy miracles and b) has a sexy AF front cover. That matters in large bookstores… so I hear.

The reader that I'm writing this for however, is the online entrepreneur who is smart. Who wants to make a huge impact on the world. Who loves money. Who wants to be rich, happy and altogether AWESOME.

But there's just one small problem.

Sales can be scary.

I hear you. Which is why I've written this book for Norma (or Norman) Normal. An online business owner or entrepreneur who has a fantastic product or service that they want to share with the world and who understands that sales skills are a necessary evil in order to help you scale your business, impact more people and pay your mortgage.

The chances are that if you're reading this book, you're also someone who likes an easy life. All of the information contained in this book, despite my casual writing style, is like sales fairy dust. Simple, easy to action information that really will help you generate as many sales as you want... without feeling like a phoney, fraud or imposter.

In this book, I'm going to give you all of the strategies, scripts and exercises that you could possibly need to learn all the sales skills that are integral to success for online entrepreneurs. I'm giving you exact blueprints, quick actions and easy to implement strategies, covering things like; running the perfect sales call, handling objections without being an arse, sales psychology, understanding how to identify your personal selling style and use it to become the sales ninja that you've always dreamed of being.

I'm going to show you the reasons that your audience aren't currently chasing down your offers and begging to pay you, which platforms to choose to help you be successful and what to do when you think you've done it all… but the strategy just isn't working.

So please, as you're reading this, make sure that you have a pen and paper to hand and that you follow along with the exercises to give yourself the best chance to make these strategies work for you.

Why me?

In life, the age old question is; how did I get here?

I had parents who were very keen for me to learn the true value of money… and so at sixteen, I trundled over to the local shopping centre to get myself a job. After landing a job at a coffee joint and miraculously lasting six hours (and seventeen cups of cold coffee) I was unceremoniously fired. Because apparently no-one in the history of employment at that well known coffee house had ever managed to make one cup of cold coffee… let alone seventeen in a row.

Dejectedly, I took my free muffin - and my own cup of cold coffee - and stood outside an international jewellery firm. The assistant manager came out and we chatted for a while about my terrible coffee, naff trainers and desire for a job that paid more than minimum wage - and an hour later I was popping my name down on a rota for all the Christmas hours that I could. It was one of the easiest interviews of my life - and my first sales job.

Jewellery sales was where I 'cut my teeth' in the sales world. And after two years of being a top performing employee (despite only being able to work twelve hours a week) I was offered the opportunity to help underperforming stores make more money. Basically, I went into stores that weren't making enough sales, fired people who weren't prepared to learn to sell differently, build brand new teams - and help them sell more stuff. By that time I was 19 and cynical, with a growing love of sales, buying psychology and pretty money hungry.

Off I trotted to university, continuing my real-life sales education - and after another three years of working hard, I was offered a job in a FTSE 250 white collar recruitment firm.

I LOVED it. It felt like everything that I had ever wanted… I got to carry a briefcase, wear heels and yell at my BlackBerry regularly. I was also one of the company's Top 20 performers within a year… out of over 5000 people in over thirty countries. Not bad for a twenty two year old.

Over the next few years, I'd work in a variety of companies and win various trips/ goodies for being a top performing sales person. I built brand new business divisions in multiple industries and disciplines. I also made a lot of money, for myself - and the companies that I worked for. Life was good.

And then I burnt out. I was tired of the corporate rat-race and couldn't find a company to 'settle' with. Having had health problems and been diagnosed with M.E, I woke up one day needing to change my life, and started up my business. Less than three years later, my business had helped over one thousand entrepreneurs in over twelve countries and was generating multi-six figures in revenue.

But let's face it. It's not really about what I have done is it?

You want to know what I've done for my clients.

People like you - who perhaps never thought that they could be good at selling, let alone enjoy it.

So let's take a look.

Over the last three and a half years I've helped normal people. Like Matthew who had a brand new business and went from making nothing in nine months… to booking over thirty thousand dollars worth of business in less than a month.

And Malaine, who went from making two - five thousand dollars a month for two years to making over thirty two thousand dollars in sixteen days.

Wonderful Helen who started a leadership movement and landed a TedX talk.

The lovely Sam who took a brand new business and made over sixteen thousand pounds in six weeks… and the amazing Jen who made over twenty four thousand pounds in six weeks.

And these are just a stand-out few from 2017 alone. I can't name each and every success story but what I can tell you is that it's not just about those who've made the 'big' numbers. It's about the sales person who signed their first corporate contract with this system. Or the entrepreneur who sold her first five thousand dollar package. Or the business owner who closed a forty thousand dollar client. It's everyone who has ever successfully practised and implemented these systems in their business or job.

These amazing people who are just like you and I. They weren't hardcore sellers. They didn't want to give up on integrity in order to make money.

They had real skills that they wanted to share with the world - and now they're working as coaches, consultants and service providers.

They're being featured in huge publications like Entrepreneur Magazine, Inspired Coach, Success, Huffington Post and more.

They're continuing their success. Working hard. And they've changed their lives irrevocably.

And they all used the sales strategies method in this book.

So let's dive into the system itself - and how you can use it to become a multi-gajillionaire.

If that's what you want.

Who is this book for?

It's just as easy (or difficult!) to sell a £20 product or service as it is to sell one at £200. Or £2000. Or £20,000.

How do I know? I've spent twelve years selling at multiple price points. Brokering multi-million dollar deals. Being the top performer in companies with people smarter than me, more attractive than me… and sometimes, even funnier than me.

But I didn't start out that way. I started out just like you. Nervous. Desperate to 'close' the deal. And ultimately? Not really closing that many sales at all.

So whether you're an entrepreneur with your own business, someone who's just made their first sale, someone who's just made their fiftieth sale or a Leonardo DiCaprio conman, this book will help you develop the right sales strategies to help you become a true sales superstar. I'm not kidding when I say that the super simple strategies in here will help you nail any sale at any price point.

In fact, as one amazing entrepreneur told my free Facebook community members in The Smart Leaders Sales Society:

Her sales system, it's so simple and yet so interesting. I cried on our interview because I was truly grateful for her generosity.

And I have to say.. I was so impressed I decided to re-watch the training and start using it again. I have closed so many high end deals since then you will not believe it.

Since November 2017, my business has sold MORE in 2.5 months than we sold in the previous year. I am not even joking. I was good at sales.

But her strategy made the sales calls more fun, allowed me to qualify better and most importantly, allowed me to pitch better and have NO objections by the time I quote the price. Jess.. I will forever be grateful for your wisdom and friendship.

- Katya Varbanova, LiveStream Queen and Founder of Peri-10K

And that's just the tip of the iceberg. So please know that regardless of what industry you're in - even if it's really 'out there' or 'saturated' or 'everyone hates being sold to' in it - this system works. And that if you believe in it, it'll work for you every time that you WANT it to.

Disclaimer #2: If you really are a 'Wolf of Wall Street', please use this book ethically. I know that I have zero power to stop your eyeballs consuming the information from my balcony - but I don't want the sales skills in here to end up in hands that are pimping drugs and terrible shiny suits.

Who is this book *not* for?

Every positive must have a negative because we thrive on opposites, so if you are someone who doesn't want to make money/ has a medically diagnosed phone allergy, can't get a phone signal without balancing at the top of a precarious branch of the rare 'GetOnThePhone' tree, then you might find this book a challenging read.

However, if I were you I'd still read it, because I promise you that by the end, even if you have to build a telephone aerial in your bedroom, you'll be dying to make successful sales calls - and tons of cash.

How to use this book correctly.

There are a couple of tips you need to ensure that you make the most of this book and no, they're probably not what you're expecting. But ultimately, as a business owner myself, and an author that wants great book reviews *hint hint, nudge nudge* I want to give you everything that you need to use this book correctly to make the income and impact that you want to in the world.

#1. Put yourself first.

Growing up, we're always taught to look out for other people. If you don't care about others or prioritise them before yourself, you're told that you're 'selfish'. Now, I'd like to think that I'm a good person. I donate to charity, volunteer and spend all of my days trying to help my community solve all of their sales problems. However, if you are a small business owner/ entrepreneur or even a salesperson working for a large conglomerate, please remember that YOU are integral to making this work. So if you're tired, burnt out and your health is shot, you're going to be no use to anyone. As you go through this book, I'd encourage you to be a little bit selfish… and follow that age old piloting instruction; 'Fit your own oxygen mask before you help others with theirs'.

Put yourself first. Your physical and mental health are integral in order to help you succeed. It's really important that during this learning process, you occasionally put this book down, go for a walk/ run/ swim and let your body and brain relax. Working 24/7 doesn't actually help you be more productive. It just ensures shitty nights of not sleeping until 2am and feeling like you're a fully paid up member of the 'hustle' club. Give yourself some free time and make sure that you put yourself and your health at the top of the priority list each day. Now I know that it's easy for me to say - because let's face it - I spent a lot of my career hustling. But I burnt out fast and at the time of writing this, can confidently say that I make more money and help my clients way more now, working a regular eight hour day with daily gym sessions and a full nine hours sleep each night. I promise you, it'll work for you too.

#2. Implement

Information without implementation is completely worthless - and I'll be the first person to step up and admit that there have been many courses, books and programmes that I've bought over the course of my business that I've read / looked at … and done absolutely nothing with.

And guess how many led to any kind of success? Zero. Not because the information wasn't good. But because my implementation / action taking skills sucked. If you're reading this book, make the decision right now that YOU are an action taker. And that you ARE going to get the best results from this book, simply by giving it a read and then using the exercises and case studies to impact your own business.

I've never had any kind of desire to have my face and name on an 'inspirational meme'… but I love hearing about the success stories that people have when using my content. So send me all of your wins and know that I'm celebrating every action taker and knowing that you'll get the results that you deserve!

#3. Be prepared to do the hard work. Daily.

Consistency equals results. And every single strategy in this book has been proven both in my business (and you can safely bet in at least 100 other businesses too!) so please, if it's not working in the way that you expect, don't blame the strategy. Get creative and reverse engineer where the problem is coming from - and be prepared to take consistent, daily action in order to see your best results. Remember, this book works, regardless of whether you're a product or service based business owner.

#4. Use the other resources available.

If you've bought this book and you have questions, you can always bring them over to my free Facebook community; The Smart Leaders Sales Society. It's easy to spot if you search it in the search bar because the cover photo has my face on it!

You can also reach out via my website and book a call with me directly so that I can help you troubleshoot any problems that you might be experiencing. Just hop over to my 'Contact' page and use the scheduler to book straight into my diary.

That's it. Basically, use the book for all it's worth, take daily action and reach out for help as and when you need it. Oh and don't burn out in the process! Now let's get rocking and rolling with the good stuff.

CHAPTER 2: WHAT TYPE OF SELLER ARE YOU?

The importance of buyer and seller styles.

In order to be better salespeople we need to understand the psychology behind buying and selling. As a complete #SalesNerd, I get really excited about helping my clients understand what kind of salesperson they are - and what kind of buying style their audience has, so that we can maximise their results and tailor the best sales strategies for their objectives.

When it comes to buying or selling, we're all different in the way that we react to pitching or being pitched to. Some of this depends on the way the sales experiences that we've already been through have gone. Did we have favourable buying experiences? Were they good experiences? Did we enjoy it? Or, alternatively, and this is what most people experience, was it a hard sale? Did it feel gross? Did it feel slimy? Did it make us, even though we purchased something, feel negative about the way that we were sold to or the way that we interacted with the person who ultimately helped us purchase the product?

In this chapter, we're going to look at the three types of sellers and buyers that we primarily see. Now, there are many more archetypes out there.

There are many different ways of buying and selling, but I've chosen to focus on the three that we see most often; aspirational, emotional and FOMO. Every other category is derived from those main three.

An important thing to think about throughout this chapter is that when we look at these categories, and we look at what kind of seller we are and what kind of buyer we are, it's integral to mention that you will not necessarily be the same kind of buyer as you are seller. You may be somebody who is a fear of missing out buyer and you really like being included in a community and you really want to be on the button when it comes down to what your peers are purchasing, but you may be an aspirational seller. You may be far enough ahead of your audience that, actually, they're looking at your lifestyle, they're looking at your relationships and thinking, "I really want that too".

It's also worth mentioning that the kind of seller you are says a lot about the way that your buyers react to you. If you have a ton of buyers in your audience who are fear of missing out buyers and you don't feel comfortable selling in that way, you need to have a serious rethink of your sales strategy. It might sound a little blunt, but if you don't sell in accordance with the buyer styles that you have access to, you'll find that you may be leaving a lot of clients (and cash) on the table by not implementing some of the basic strategies behind those psychological buying behaviours.

Ultimately, not listening to these buying signals can mean that your audience miss out on getting the results that they really want, or worse, they buy from somebody who doesn't have as much integrity as you and who perhaps can't help them get the same results you can just because they listened to their audience's behaviour, and used their sales strategy to respond accordingly.

Over time, you may want to integrate different sales styles - and it's important to note that your selling style will evolve over time. There are certain products / services in my business that sell much better using a FOMO sales approach, than an aspirational one and vice versa. Throughout this chapter, you'll find that you might identify strongly with one or two sales types; I naturally fall into the aspirational/ FOMO sales categories… and I find emotional selling doesn't match my personality and doesn't appeal to the majority of my audience.

There are many positives and some negatives (!) to each of these styles. The important thing to recognise is that you need to be responsible for your sales integrity. Integrity is always up to you. Do not take clients that you can't handle. Do not take clients that you can't deliver to. Do not sell in a way that makes you feel uncomfortable, and don't sell in a way that's going to make your audience feel gross or slimy.

That's not what it's about. The sales experience should be really positive, and you should be leaning on your skills, your expertise, and looking at what it is that is inspiring or motivating your audience to buy from you and leveraging that. Done with integrity, there is nothing wrong with that at all. So lets dig into this chapter and into the three main selling styles. We'll look at how you can identify yourself as a specific type of buyer so that you can choose to buy in an informed way and the three types of sellers that you may be and how you can really use those archetypes to sell effectively, to sell with integrity and, more importantly, to sell successfully.

Does my personality affect my sales style?

Before we dive straight into the sales styles, I just want to hit pause for a second. One of the toughest things about sales is that your personality makes a huge difference to your selling success - and one of the questions that I am always hearing is;

"But Jess, I'm an introvert. Introverts can't sell... can they?"

The simple answer honestly, is that anyone really can sell. It doesn't matter about your gender, hair colour, race or religion. And whether you're introverted or extroverted, there is a sales style that will work for you. So if you've been reading along feeling slightly concerned that you're not a tequila slamming, table dancing, karaoke crashing extrovert... then it's okay. You can absolutely use any of the strategies in this book; it's just about knowing which ones resonate most with you, and which of your personality traits you want to use to help you sell successfully.

Let's just grab a quick peek at the definition of introvert/ extrovert. In today's society, we typically make assumptions about what introverts and extroverts do and how they act. We assume that introverts are quiet, shy and don't like speaking up or confrontation. And we also assume that extroverts are exactly how I described above; life and soul of the party, aren't happy unless they're surrounded by people and always the biggest personality in the room.

The true definition of an introvert however, is someone who tends to focus on their own internal thoughts and feelings, rather than the external things around them. And an extrovert is a person who is primarily concerned with external or objective considerations. If we turn this to sales, it becomes a conversation about where we take our energy from.

So for example, an introvert is someone who is drained by the energy of lots of people in the room. An extrovert is someone who thrives on the company of others - and that company restores their energy.

(Anyone else feeling like I suddenly hit the 'woo' button?!)

But seriously, the strategies that introverts and extroverts use to sell are actually no different. But their offers are. Because a large group programme or running a huge ten thousand person Facebook group would be incredibly overwhelming to someone who identifies as an introvert. Introverts tend to thrive on deeper relationships and working in small groups or 1:1 with their customers. Typically, we see a lot of graphic designers/ web designers and high end coaches who tend to be introverts. They enjoy seeing a project through, paying attention to detail and having a good relationship with one point of contact.

An extrovert however, tends to be someone who wants to build a huge personal brand. Someone who thrives off of the energy of running a large community or large group programmes. Typically, you'll find that big social media influencers tend to be extroverted. They enjoy the 'ping' of Facebook notifications and being super present in their communities.

Let's take a look at some of the differences in the potential community development and promotion strategies used by introverts and extroverts.

Introverts:

• Unlikely to want to market or promote in hundreds of large Facebook communities - or run a large community yourself.

• Is more likely to avoid live content such as Facebook live, and enjoys pre-recorded content like; recorded video, podcasting, blogging… something where they can be slightly removed from their end users.

• Prefers audience members to reach out 1:1. Many introverted sellers have extremely successful email lists. They communicate really well via email and establish solid relationships with people in their community who will often reach out in response to their email marketing to thank them or share experiences.

• Likes to provide high end 1:1 / intimate group experiences.

Extroverts:

• Is / Wants to be a social media influencer.

• Enjoys building big communities and is an active community manager.

- Enjoys sharing their 'behind the scenes' moments and daily life.
- Prolific content creator on 'live' platforms (platforms that move in real time like Facebook Live, Instagram, Twitter etc)
- Likes to create large group programmes/ memberships.

Exercise: Are you introverted or extroverted? Does your personality match the offers that you are currently putting out to your audience? What kind of platform/ presence do you want to have for your visibility?

Aspirational Selling

The first sales style (and probably the most common for salespeople specifically focusing on marketing themselves in the online space,) is aspirational selling. Now, when we talk about aspirational selling, we're looking at salespeople who use their current lives/ businesses/ health/ relationships to sell to you. They're the people that you want to emulate and that showcase their achievements in a way that helps you to realise that it can happen for you too. You'll find that most aspirational sellers are operating as; coaches, consultants, lifestyle/ travel bloggers or luxury product creators, but like all the sales types, can be found across many different industries.

Generally, the easiest way to identify aspirational selling is looking at how it makes you feel.

"Does this make me feel like I would like this person's life, this person's business? Do I feel like that is something that I want to aspire to or that motivates me?"

Typical examples that you see of this are really popular with online business coaches, who market the 'laptop lifestyle' Typically, their branding usually reflects regular travel, drool worthy photos and luxury experiences.

To their ideal client, their life looks pretty close to perfect. That tends to be one of the key signs of an aspirational seller, somebody who is using their life and the way that their life works or the way that their business works to be aspirational, to inspire, to motivate, and to encourage people to buy from them.

So, what happens when this person sells? Well, it's pretty simple. They build up their content with photos/ experiences that their ideal clients aspire to have or achieve. You'll find that most aspirational sellers in the online space are prolific when it comes to posting on social media, and they'll tend to favour the visual platforms such as Instagram or Pinterest which makes it easier to showcase their lifestyle and any behind the scenes elements that they want to share with their audience to make them feel included.

You'll also find that aspirational sellers really focus on the life that they're experiencing now as a result of their particular breakthrough or transformation so they will Instagram photos of their life. They will put out content that talks about something that they know is really going to resonate with their ideal clients. Sometimes you'll see photos of brand-new Chanel bags and captions that say, "Oh my goodness. I walked into Chanel today, and I just bought this. Life is good, because I was able to buy this. I didn't have to worry about it. It's something that I'd always dreamed of and never really thought would happen, but now it has."

This content strategy, matched alongside regular offers for programmes/ products or services that helps the customer to achieve the same lifestyle/ health goals/ relationship goals/ look are all indicative of an aspirational seller. The sales pitches that an aspirational seller uses will be focused around what they have achieved and how you can achieve the same. They're directly looking for people who identify with the life that they're living or the business that they have or the fitness regime that they love, and they are selling you that based on what it has done for them.

Integrity wise, you tend to find that most aspirational sellers will be selling with integrity, because they're simply showcasing their achievements and lifestyle to demonstrate what is possible for their audience to achieve through living it out in real time.

Now, where aspirational selling can go wrong is when we see false examples… there are plenty of them around on the internet, but generally, if it looks too good to be true (private jets and three thousand Lamborghini's on the front drive) then it probably is. Always do your due diligence when it comes to aspirational sellers - and remember that your audience will do the same.

It's also important to remember that in order to be an aspirational seller, you don't have to be a fit twenty-something who's crazy about branded fashion and diamonds. Aspirational sellers can be anyone seen as any expert with a lifestyle or qualifications that the buyer desires to have. Think about hot-shot lawyer Harvey Specter in the US TV series, Suits. He's an expert in his industry, attractive and drives an Aston Martin DB9. Girls love him and the guys want to be him. And if he was to sell anything? He'd find it easy to be an aspirational seller (or a total shark!) for sure.

So how do you know if you are an aspirational seller?

- Are you living a lifestyle that other people desire? Or do you have key elements in your life/ health/ relationship that others want?
- Are you someone who wants to become a social media influencer? You either have (or want) a large and engaged following who are interested in your every move.
- Are you selling a product or service that is designed to help your clients achieve the same things that you have achieved?

If you're a YES to two or more, it's quite likely that you are an aspirational seller. Just remember not to judge your aspirational selling on the key influencer that you admire. Comparisonitis will kill your sales - and you can be just as aspirational as key influencers… even if you haven't made millions/ don't have the perfect body/ still have a way to go before you hit all of your goals. Aspirational selling is about being two or three steps ahead of your ideal client and showing them that their dreams really are possible.

Now, as I briefly mentioned, if you're an aspirational buyer, you are somebody who typically purchases based on wanting to achieve a certain level in your business/ lifestyle/ other key area that somebody else has achieved. You can often tell if your audience is made up of primarily aspirational buyers if they want to be let into your life or the 'behind the scenes' element to your business. Aspirational buyers are also usually loyal purchasers and referrers - and they'll want to keep the aspirational seller close during their journey to the top!

Case Study: Kylie Jenner

One of the easiest ways to recognise aspirational sellers, is to look at celebrities. And one of the most famous, aspirational sales style celebrities from 2017 is Kylie Jenner. At just 20 years old, Kylie Jenner has managed to turn her $29 lipstick company into a multi-million dollar beauty empire, primarily through aspirational selling.

According to WWD, Kylie's online lipstick business netted her over $420m in 2017 - and it is thought that if her sales and business continue their skyward trajectory, that the company will be a billion dollar firm by 2022. She also became the youngest celebrity to hit the Forbes list, as well as having multiple sold out, same day launches for her beauty products. So let's look at what makes Kylie so popular - and how she uses aspirational selling to her advantage.

Kylie Jenner is a prolific Instagrammer. In fact at the point of writing this, she has over 100 million followers. One hundred million people who all watch her stories. Who watch her live videos. Who look at all of her posts and get excited about her products. Her social media feed is made up primarily of magazine covers where she is the featured star, her own brand cosmetics and pictures of her in amazing locations, wearing high ticket clothing and her own brand make up.

All of these things appeal to her target demographic; girls in their late teens/ early twenties who also dream of being a 'star', who want the luxury lifestyle, who want to look like Kylie Jenner. And so when they scroll her feed and they see pictures of her on catwalks, at premieres or with her celebrity friends, they want to emulate that - and their subconscious tells them that the easiest way to do it is to buy her products.

So remember, if you're an aspirational seller, you need to be sharing the parts of life that your audience want to see and wish they had for themselves. Alongside regular 'behind the scenes' content and sales pitches. You'll need to build a strong personal brand and be unafraid to diversify into new markets, partnerships and joint ventures… but don't worry. Because if you're an aspirational seller who actually gets your audience the result that they want? They'll be super loyal - and always want to purchase your products!

Emotional

Okay... moving onto my least favourite sales style. Emotional selling. It's one that gets a really bad rap in the industry, especially in the online space where it's become much more prevalent. Now, this is a sales style that you don't tend to see that often in the corporate world, and the reason for that is that corporate businesses tend to rely much more heavily on testimonials, reputation or proven results.

Corporate companies don't always sit entirely in any of these categories as buyers or sellers. The reason behind that is that most corporate companies have large sales and procurement teams that are full of different people and different characteristics, brought together to help achieve one specific goal.

Some industries will lean more towards a sales style; particularly with the fashion industry, luxury brands or jewellery. You'll find that these types of businesses, will lean towards an aspirational selling style for their audience because they want them to look at their clothes/ products and imagine themselves wearing them and becoming the person in the advert!

Emotional selling however, is not a sales style that you'll see in the corporate world... unless you happen to have a salesperson who can turn tears on demand! Emotional selling has become an almost exclusive sales style to businesses run by solopreneurs/ entrepreneurs and anyone who has focused on building their business based on their personal brand.

Now I'm the first person to admit that I'm not the biggest fan of the emotional sell… so I'm going to try and be fair in this chapter, but you might have to cut me a little slack! I'm not a fan of the emotional sale for a couple of reasons;

1. Personally, I am not an emotional buyer. We're going to talk about the qualities in detail later. Being an emotional buyer, just as an FYI, does not mean that you cry your way through the purchase. In terms of my buying personality, I'm not an emotional buyer. I don't buy because I'm emotionally connected in some way to the person selling the product or service or because I feel that if I buy from them, I'll be their new best friend. I don't buy for that reason. I'm an aspirational buyer. I buy because I want what that person has achieved or what that person has done in terms of results. Or I can be a fear of missing out buyer. I can buy because my colleagues and peers are doing things, and I know that if they are doing those things, it would probably be quite a good step up or challenge for me, too.

2. The way that this style has been misused to target potentially vulnerable buyers repulses me. (Wow, that came out more bluntly than I expected!)

In the online space specifically, we've seen a rise of emotional sales tactics over the last three years, certainly, the last three years that I've been in business. One of the reasons that it does get such a bad reputation is because people misuse this sales strategy. It is the most common misused sales strategy in the online space at the moment.

The reason for that is emotional selling and emotional buying is defined by somebody being triggered to buy something as a result of having a deep emotional connection with that person and, therefore, with their product or service. Now, in a world of integrity-based sales, that's a really positive thing. We're going along the lines of we buy from people we know, like, and trust.

Now obviously, it's really easy to increase somebody's trust in you and to build a deeper connection and relationship with a person or prospective buyer when you are able to show them some level of vulnerability and when you are able to take yourself off the pedestal and connect them deeper with your story, your mission, your vision, and your purpose.

When you're selling with integrity, emotional sales is a good strategy for people building a personal brand, because it means that you can align people together with the mission, vision and your purpose that you are trying to achieve at the same time as helping them build a better relationship with you. It also helps them to buy safe in the knowledge that they're doing the right thing. However, it does get misused, and the online world has had a spate, over the last couple of years, of people pimping their pain for profit. For me, this is where the line gets blurry (and where I get frustrated with the clear misuse of the strategy!)

Integrity isn't always a word that we hear in conjunction with sales, but I can assure you that there are some great sales people out there *cough cough* who don't believe in lying or manipulating their potential clients. Emotional selling can lend itself unfortunately well to manipulation - and playing with the emotions of your prospective client, so it's imperative that if you are an emotional seller, that you act with integrity and ensure that your prospective client is always protected during the sales process.

So how do we identify emotional selling - and are there any positive aspects to it?

- Emotional selling is a polarising sales style. Bad salespeople will use it to pimp their pain for profit and you'll be able to spot them a mile off.

They'll be the salespeople who sell using a painful/ traumatic event that they're currently experiencing in real time, in order to sell their latest programme or service. Great emotional sellers will share vulnerably - but they'll focus on the lessons learned, rather than the cause of the trauma, in order to make their sale.

- When done well, emotional selling can be very powerful. It can establish strong relationships. It can establish the know, like, trust factor. It can establish true leadership. It can show your audience that you are vulnerable. It can show them that you're still a leader. It can show them that you're still knowledgeable. It can help them trust you. It can help them build a deeper connection with you.When done in a manipulative manner, it can be very, very detrimental to your audience in that they may be buying things that are not right for them, and therefore, they don't get the results that they want.

Now, the difficulty is that emotional selling and aspirational selling can often look very similar. If you're an emotional buyer, and that means that you buy primarily based on someone's story and the relationship you have with them rather than necessarily looking at all of the pros and cons and thinking, "Do I really need to make this investment right now?"

As an emotional buyer, you look at the person and at their story. You look at the relationship you have with them, and you say, "Based on those things, I want to make the purchase for this course or product or service." In terms of selling, aspirational selling and emotional selling actually look fairly similar, because as we talked about in the last chapter, aspirational selling is very much about utilising your personal brand. It's very much about showing people your life. It's about showing them the present, the here, the now.

So is emotional selling, but the difference is that your audience will be left with an entirely different taste in their mouth if it is done in the wrong way. So, for example, aspirational selling done the right way makes somebody think, “wow, this person is living in the present. They're living in the here and now. I really want to buy from them, because I want to achieve the same results or have the same lifestyle right now”. Emotional selling, when done in the right way, makes people say, "Ah, I know this person. I trust them. I like them. I'm going to ask them whether or not this product or service is right for me, and if they say yes, I'm going to purchase it."

Emotional selling is not about having an ill-informed audience. It's about opening up the process for your audience to make an informed decision about whether this is the right option for them. So we still welcome questions. It's still about educating your audience. It's still about the making the right decision for them.

Emotional selling done in the wrong way will leave your audience feeling something like this. Let's look at a typical example; (Usually seen on Facebook)

*** Vulnerable Post Alert ***

Insert sad situation here.

I'm currently experiencing the worst time of my life. [Insert break-up/ bereavement/ some kind of loss]. In fact, [insert form of blame; another person, the universe etc] has made me feel [insert sad adjective of choice].

The good news is though, that I'm going to [insert phrase about overcoming the situation] and I can help YOU do that too [insert sales pitch]

Now don't get me wrong, I am a naturally cynical person. But I'm also a person who is empathetic to certain causes. I donate to charity. I hate bullies. I am a huge animal lover. What I intensely dislike about emotional selling is when a bad salesperson manipulates the values of a certain charity or feeling, to share 'vulnerably' and then makes a pitch off the back of it.

And yes, I'm making a mental note to finish this chapter and scrub my skin with salt…

Bad emotional selling is designed to be manipulative, it's very much focused on pain.

Everything is focused on the pain or the trauma of a specific situation. With positive emotional selling or even aspirational selling in some parts, it's about focusing on the learning experience.

So the difference between a good emotional seller, somebody that's selling with integrity and somebody that is aware of the power they hold when it comes to the relationships they've built with their community and the difference between somebody who is manipulating people for money is that the good salesperson will only be sharing the learning experience. Not simply pimping their pain for profit and sharing a painful experience, a traumatic experience, for nothing other than sympathy and sales.

Now, you've got to make your own mind up about how that comes across for you. There are some people who really do have tragic stories. I've met many people both online and offline who've had terribly traumatic pasts who have gone on to be incredibly inspirational people. There are other people who I have met who have, for want of a better phrase, pimped their pain for profit and who have not delivered as they've promised.

After all, with great power comes great responsibility - and it can be very irresponsible (not to mention dangerous) to mess with the emotions of your audience. Long term, if your audience feel like they're being manipulated through trauma, they'll leave your community - and they'll tell lots of other people about the lack of integrity that they've experienced.

Personally, my feeling is that if you are an emotional seller, your responsibility is always to leave your door open so that your audience can ask you questions. If you're an emotional seller, if most of your content is around your story, your learning experiences, your breakthroughs, your journey, expressing your vulnerability, sharing your celebrations, that kind of thing, please make sure that when you are selling, the door is open for your audience to ask questions. When they come to you and honestly say, "Hey, Jess, is this really the right decision for me?" you assess it honestly and you say yes or no based on your expert opinion rather than your mortgage payment.

In all honesty, the emotional seller has possibly the most power out of any kind of sales strategy out there or any kind of sales psychology because they have built a really strong foundation to a relationship. People want to continue that. You do have the power to say no to clients if it's not right for them. Now, if you're an emotional buyer and you know that you connect with people really strongly and you think that you really want to work with a specific person or business, it is your job to do your due diligence.

Not necessarily around the person, because the likelihood is if you're an emotional buyer, you've been following them for a long time. You know them well. You have experienced highs and lows with them. You've been on the journey, and you feel really good about this person. You've got to be doing due diligence around what they're selling.

So asking yourself the question, "do I really need this product, programme, or service right now? Am I actually going to put it into practice? I.e., am I going to implement what I'm learning? Am I going to use it? Is it something that's going to generate some kind of ROI in my life, in my business, in my health, et cetera?"

If the answer to any of those is no, take a step back and think about whether you're ready to buy now or whether, actually, you need to wait for the right product that they're selling to come along.

Now, I hate being a Debbie Downer. Emotional selling, when done well and when done with integrity, is one of the best types of sales experiences out there. It can make people feel incredibly connected to you. It can make people feel like they have this really amazing relationship with the seller.

And as a seller, you do generate these incredible connections that you do not always see from other types of selling perspective. You just have to be really sensible about how you use it.

You have to have clear boundaries about who you will or will not work with. And you have to have absolute integrity when somebody comes to you and asks whether or not they need to work with you.

The definition of an emotional buyer is that they will want to ask your opinion. They will want your opinion, because they value you. They value your opinion, and they want you to reassure them that what they're doing is what's best for them because of the relationship they have with you. So just be very aware of that when you're an emotional seller or an emotional buyer. Responsibility needs to be taken on both sides to ensure a long-term, successful buying/ selling relationship.

FOMO

The Fear of Missing Out or FOMO selling style is arguably the most popular in the world… and it means that a lot of us (including me!) have been trained into becoming FOMO buyers. In other words, in a world full of instant gratification and social media accessibility, we fear missing out on new/ special offers.

I'm writing this book in December, traditionally the biggest retail revenue month of the year. Stores are selling items at full price… and yet we know, that in January, most of us will be heading out to shop in the January sales. Now yes, there's the odd occasion that you're going to get an absolute bargain on an item that you've been coveting, usually big ticket home goods like televisions or sofas, but the reality is that the majority of the time you're giving shops money for end of season line skirts and shirts that you didn't like enough to buy at full price.

(Please tell me that I'm not the only one who does this?!)

The reason is super simple. We worry about missing out. And with the rise in technology and cyber stalking via paid advertising, shops (and potential purchases) follow us around the internet with big neon signs announcing;

"Ending Soon"

"Buy Now… or Miss Out"

Companies are also employing the use of different pieces of software to increase our feelings of scarcity and FOMO. Countdown timers are becoming widely used, alongside huge banners/ pop-ups on websites to help increase the feelings of urgency that a buyer feels and make them come to a quicker buying decision.

These are just some of the FOMO selling techniques that we see regularly, but if you're a FOMO seller, it's not just dependent on the technology that you use, but also your personality and the audience that you have. In fact, it's dependent on your following, because if you have zero following, it's really hard for you to create a campaign where you create that urgency and that FOMO, because you don't have anyone there to sell to!

If you're a FOMO seller, it's quite likely that you have an engaged community / following that has already demonstrated that they want to buy from you. You might have a public forum for this tribe; a Facebook Community or similar, and you'll be defined by certain characteristics and the sales strategies that you employ. For example, as a FOMO seller, you love urgency. You love publicly highlighting when people have bought into your product, programme, or service and you understand that the public accountability or celebration, will help attract / convert other buyers.

Now, there are ways of doing this, and some of the most common ones that you will see online are in Facebook groups. They usually appear if somebody has purchased a programme/ product or service and the seller will welcome them publicly into the programme. I use this method a lot when it comes to selling group programmes or passive products. This method is super successful for a couple of reasons;

1. It makes the new purchaser feel good about their purchase. They're being publicly congratulated and it reduces any potential buyers remorse. That's really positive, because as a buyer, they feel validated, valued and identified publicly as an action taker. It solidifies for the buyer that they made the right decision; that you are confident in them and their results.
2. It also publicly shows prospective buyers that other people (their peers) are purchasing your products or services and gives them confidence. As the seller, it shows that people are purchasing your products and services and that they are publicly happy for the world to see that they are identifying with what you're selling and that they are ready to take action. Perfect for the people who consider themselves the buyers peers / colleagues or people within the same network who want to achieve similar results or hit similar goals.

From FOMO sellers, we typically see the use of urgency and, during launch times, consistent promotion of the key motivators for the buyer to make the purchase. Interestingly, FOMO sellers don't have to be purely live launch driven. You can be a FOMO seller with an evergreen product or service. In fact, a strategy that works really well if you have a product or a service that is run on an evergreen basis would be ensuring that your course/ programme on-boarding has the buyer request access to join the private community for your paid service by going into your free community and saying, "Hey, I just need to request access to this great course or this private Facebook community for this course."

That works well because it drives traffic to your evergreen funnel. When somebody's coming in and saying, "Hey, I just bought this, and I'm really excited, and I want to get into the private paid community"it means that other people are seeing it and going, "What am I missing out on? What am I not seeing? Maybe I haven't seen the programme. Maybe I haven't seen the funnel that leads to it, and I really want to now."

A word of caution for FOMO sellers however is that if you employ traditional FOMO techniques all the time, you'll find that your audience gets burned. You can't do the same things all the time with a fear of missing out strategy, because actually, people just get desensitised. They don't care anymore. They're like, "Oh, whatever. Another person's bought it. That's great. Cool. Whatever."

As time goes by, you may find that it's not working in the same way. So people who are fear of missing out sellers tend to have open-cart launches, so they open the cart on a specific day, and they close the cart on another specific day so that they can drive as much urgency as they want to that programme or service.

Now, it doesn't necessarily mean that the programme or service is run on a live basis, but it does mean that the launch for it is live. Everything is live for the launch. Think about key performers in the online marketing space. Jeff Walker for example, sells his Product Launch Formula (TM) course twice a year. The course itself is already created, but he uses open/ close cart dates, plus some incredible affiliates to help drive as much traffic and urgency to his launch as possible.

So FOMO sellers are defined by; driving purposeful urgency, using technology to support the scarcity drive and using their tribes / communities to support new sales. But what does a FOMO buyer look like?

If you are a fear of missing out type buyer (or are lucky enough to have FOMO buyers in your community), you might actually thrive on some of the experiences that I've already highlighted. FOMO buyers tend to be easy to spot in that they'll tend to exhibit some specific behaviours;

- If one of their friends or peers buys into something, they will probably buy into it too, because they want to get the same results that their friend/ peer does.
- FOMO buyers don't want to be left behind. They are usually somebody who checks the

countdown timer regularly. Interestingly enough, people who are fear of missing out buyers do not tend to be early bird buyers. Just a fun fact for you there. Statistically, people who have a fear of missing out tend to buy at the last minute. What will happen, psychologically, is that their brain will be thinking, "We need something to tip us over the edge. Give us the trigger. Send us the message. Give us the last sign." If you're a fear of missing out buyer, then you really do wait for that countdown timer to hit, and you are somebody who will buy in those last hours.

Now this is all super helpful if you're a FOMO seller or you have a community (or people within it) who embody these kinds of buying qualities, because it helps you utilise all aspects of your launch; especially those final hours!

Although you might be thinking, "Ugh, there's no point. I'm really tired. Launching is hard," you actually are at a pivotal point in your launch where you can pick up quite a few last-minute sales so it's really important to recognise these elements. If you're a fear of missing out kind of buyer, you need to watch out for the kinds of triggers that are going to help support you making a buying decision. If you are a fear of missing out seller or you have buyers in your community who are triggered by the fear of missing out qualities, start putting preparations in place for your launches so that you can catch those people even right at the end of the process.

CHAPTER 3: CHOOSING YOUR SALES PLATFORM

What platform is right for you?

The internet is possibly one of my favourite places to hang out as a sales nerd and avid people watcher. Along with coffee shops, Zumba classes and the cinema… because all of these environments bring me the two things that I love the most.

1. The ability to stalk other peoples sale's techniques.
2. Time to watch how people interact and behave in certain situations or places.

Now I promise that I'm not just some kind of oddball… but I do love sales psychology. And for the last 3.5 years, I've been fascinated by the fact that the internet has allowed me to grow a business where I have access to more potential customers than ever before. And where I can carve out my own niche, show up authentically and still make the money that I want online.

When I started my sales business, I was overwhelmed at the vast numbers of people using social media everyday. In fact, social media has allowed me to know my audience better than ever before - and has given me the ability to sell to over seven billion people across all seven continents.

For a saleswoman who was once restricted to selling to organisations in specific post (zip) codes, it was both a joy and a curse.

You see, the first thing that a career in corporate sales teaches you, is that you've got to niche. Whether it's based on who your ideal client is and the characteristics that they have, the location that you're able to work in, industry, sector, discipline or even language. The point is, having too many birds to try and catch means that none end up in the proverbial hand.

The first thing that I look at with my clients is how and where they're showing up online. Which platforms have they chosen to represent themselves on? How are they selling to those prospects? How often? And the common theme seems to be that people jump into online businesses and feel the e-x-p-a-n-s-i-o-n that they wouldn't normally feel in a corporate company.

Suddenly, they're working for themselves! They can be as strict / loose on time management and KPIs as they want. They can work with clients in any country that they want. They can sell any type of product or service that they want… But if you've ever been to a 'Round the World, All You Can Eat' buffet, you'll know that too many choices kill your ability to make quick and effective decisions.

So I want to share why choosing the right platform is so important in order to become a top salesperson in your business. It's not just about looking at which platform has the best adverts; but is in fact, a simple decision making process, based on your seller and personality types.

Grab a cup of tea whilst I walk you through the platforms and the reasons that they make great sales platforms - depending on you and how you want to show up and sell! I have to preface this with the fact that I've built my business and used multiple platforms… I've mastered them one at a time and now use them each for different things. Please don't fall into the trap of thinking that in order to make sales, you have to be everywhere. As John Lee Dumas, Founder of Entrepreneur on Fire said at the YouPreneur Summit, "You've got to go one inch wide and one mile deep". Use that strategy when it comes to starting (and selling) on social media and you'll find that you're much more successful, much more quickly.

Facebook

Let's start with Facebook. Honestly, I've always had a love/ hate relationship with Facebook. I joined the platform back in 2011… and spent most of my teenage years worrying about whether or not someone had 'liked' my status update, and spent hours trying to be as witty as possible (without being so smart that the boys at school wouldn't get it!)

For many new online entrepreneurs, Facebook is touted as the simplest platform to get started on - and it can be. There are over seven billion people in the world and it's estimated that more than one billion people per month are active Facebook users. Isn't that crazy?! In this world, technology has bridged gaps that even travel hasn't always been able to - and in the world of business / sales, it's giving us access to more customers than we could ever possibly serve.

Most people already have a Facebook account that they can sell from. Now there are good ways of doing this - and ways that will get you unfriended super quickly, so make sure that you read through to the online sales 'net-etiquette' chapter so that you're not reprimanded as a spammer! Facebook is probably the easiest of the social media platforms to set up and sell from for the simple reasons that a) most people are already on Facebook and familiar with the platform and b) that Mark Zuckerberg has created a phenomenal social platform that encourages community building, engagement and monetisation. It's pretty exceptional - and despite not always being a Facebook fan-girl, I have to say that it did change my life… and the trajectory of my business forever.

If you're going to get started with sales on Facebook, there are three surefire ways to make it happen.

1. Sell from your personal profile.

The official Facebook rules are that your personal profile cannot be used for business purposes - and I completely agree that your personal profile should be personal. However, you've got to take into account the 80/20 rule, otherwise known as Pareto Law. I think of it like this. Eighty percent of the time, I show up as me on my personal profile. I have my holiday pictures, bad bikini shots and day to day photos of my dog. Twenty percent of the time however, I'll have done something that I'm actually really proud of… and just like when I was in my corporate job, I'll let the Facebook world know that I'm pleased. For example;

"I'm going to be on TV tonight!"

Or…

"I am so excited for [Insert Client Name] who made over £XXXX in XXX days!"

Those are things that I'm excited about. They're things/ experiences that I'd share if I still had my job - and Facebook is okay with that. It's inadvertently promoting (because hey, who doesn't want to work with someone whose clients get amazing results?!) but it's okay within Facebook's terms and conditions. What they don't want you to do is constantly be spamming your friends with offers for Tupperware, links to the latest beauty craze… but we'll talk about that in a moment! Selling from your personal profile works best if you're happy to share the 'behind the scenes' or 'real life' stuff when it comes to your business. If you're someone who's happy to share regularly and show up with edutainment (educational and informative content!) then you can sell from your personal profile - but only in conjunction with at least one other method so that you don't get booted by Zuckerberg!

2. Groups.

Can I get some kind of hand heart here for Facebook communities? I freaking love them. Starting a Facebook group was one of the best things that I ever did for my business. Now don't get me wrong, I go through phases of loving it, wanting to change it and being supremely frustrated by it. That's because I'm human. But my Facebook community generated over 42% of my revenue in 2017 - certainly nothing to sniff at! So how do Facebook groups work when it comes to selling?

It's pretty simple, setting up a free Facebook community helps you become a leader in your space and gives you leave to deliver value and expertise to your community - and to sell to them with integrity. Again, the 80/20 rule applies here; eighty percent of the time, you should be focused on showing up and supporting your community, giving value and educating them … and twenty percent of the time you should be showing up unashamedly and selling your heart out! I talk more about how you can give great value but also help your buyers become early decision makers (and help them to buy from you super quickly during the process!) in the next chapter. It really falls down to a delicate balancing act between giving value and being clear on your sales boundaries - but we'll dive into that later.

In order to sell successfully using Facebook groups, you need to do a few things;

- Figure out the purpose of your group. The mistake that most people make when creating a Facebook group is that they only want to make money. Now of course, your group has to sit in line with your business and must generate profit… but in order to build a true community of die-hard, raving fans, it's important that your community has a wider purpose. My free Facebook community, The Smart Leaders Sales Society, is focused on supporting leaders and future industry leaders learn simple sales techniques that add more profit to their bottom line.

- Be prepared to show up. Groups (and especially new communities) require a lot of your time and energy. Simply starting one isn't enough. You've got to show up and add value regularly (even if you feel like you're just hearing crickets!) Plan out a clear value schedule for your community so that people know when they can show up and learn, how to ask questions and how to benefit other community members. The easiest way for me to do this was to create a short welcome video outlining my expectations for the group, my live training schedule and my expectations of the people who join. I decided to hold regular free live trainings - and in 2017 alone, spent over 400 hours on free trainings... That doesn't mean that YOU need to. In fact, in 2018, I've committed to hosting one free live training per week and daily written content that helps my members stay engaged, but doesn't overwhelm them or teach them bad business habits that lead to burn out!
- Sell regularly. This sounds simple, but most new group owners fall into the trap of serving all the time and never selling. One of the most-asked questions that I hear is;

'How many members do I need before I can sell?' The answer is, that it's not about the numbers. You should be showing up and selling regularly so that you train your audience into buying - and normalise the sales experience so that they begin to enjoy it!

To sell effectively from a Facebook community, you also need to be happy to lead it. Communities often take on lives/ cultures of their own, and it's up to you to cultivate the best environment that you can. That will ensure that your audience become raving fans, quick buyers - and that they stick around and refer the group to other prospective clients too!

3. Facebook Business Pages.

So at the time of writing this, Mark Zuckerberg announced some big changes to the way that Facebook business pages were going to work. People have often moaned that the organic reach on Facebook business pages is really low - but we do have to remember, that Facebook is a 'pay to play' environment. Zuckerberg has built his business on monetising the ginormous community that he has built, through charging companies for advertising - and it's worked phenomenally well.

The Facebook business page gives you two sales options; organic and paid. Organic simply means that you'll use your Facebook business page to cultivate a following (without using paid traffic) and that you'll sell regularly to that audience. Paid traffic is about using Facebook advertising to increase your reach and put more people into your funnel. Now you might already be falling down the 'My Facebook Business Page Sucks' rabbit hole… and honestly, I can tell you that they still are super effective when used correctly.

The new rules that Facebook are setting around clickbait content and the desire to create more engagement is actually fantastic news for people who want to sell from a Facebook business page. In fact, one of my incredible clients, Liz, is the queen of Facebook Ads… and her business page gets more engagement than most groups. The difference between the way that she runs it however, and the way that most people run their pages, is that she shows up regularly with interesting and engaging content (including live video) and monetises it through selling regularly. She sticks to Zuckerberg's rule and creates content that her audience actually want to see - and so it shows up regularly in their newsfeed.

Put simply, the new rules just mean that you'll need to cultivate a solid following and post interesting and engaging content so that it's seen regularly in your prospects newsfeed. So don't be dull - make sure that if you're using the Facebook business page, you're operating within the 80/20 rule. Eighty percent of the time, show up and educate or show the 'behind the scenes'... and twenty percent of the time, SELL!

To be a successful Facebook business page seller, you need to be very clear on who your ideal client is - and the message that speaks to them. It will involve a lot of foundational work but can gain traction and sales quickly. You'll also find that Facebook prioritises video as a medium - so try and include video content to improve your opportunities to speak to your audience. Successful Facebook business page users are generally sharing regular edutainment content, like the idea of one-way conversation / using FB as more of a blogging type platform and who are looking to scale their businesses with paid traffic later down the line.

Instagram

Instagram is rising quickly in the race for social media domination. With over 100 million users per month (and having been recently acquired by Facebook!) Instagram is appearing on thousands of smartphone screens every day. Now I'll be totally honest, before starting my business, I didn't really get Instagram. It was just people sharing pretty pictures… or funny memes. I didn't really see how it could be monetised.

However, as the years went by, I realised that there were masses of people on Instagram who simply didn't spend time on Facebook. And it's important to know that when you're picking your social media platform of choice, it's not just about where you want to spend your time, it's also about where your ideal clients are spending theirs!

My client Sam for example, is the queen of Instagram. She has been known to set up brand new accounts and grow them to over ten thousand followers in less than three months! Her clients are primarily entrepreneurs who want to get visible… and Instagram gives them another platform to showcase their expertise.

Now Instagram is what I like to call a 'driver' platform. There are ways of building relationships on Instagram - but there's no way to build a community. It's more of a visual/ blog platform - so what I like to do, is move people over from Instagram to a platform where we can build a deeper relationship. I direct people across to my Facebook community, where we can have a two way conversation or to my email list, where they can get regular value and reply at their leisure!

As a platform, Instagram is simple to monetise and works well - once you've built your following and engagement. However, initial sales through

Instagram tend to be lower ticket than from Facebook Groups/ LinkedIn. That's not necessarily an issue, as long as you have a funnel past the initial low ticket product. If you can up-sell into a premium programme, then you'll increase your lifetime customer value - and the benefit that your customer gets from you.

If you're someone who enjoys curating amazing images and creating cool captions / short videos, then Instagram could be a fantastic platform for you!

LinkedIn

It's no secret that LinkedIn is one of my favourite platforms. It might not be as intuitive as Facebook… or as pretty as Instagram. But when it comes to sales, LinkedIn competes for the top spot with ease! During the first year of my business, LinkedIn generated over 70% of my revenue! That's a vast amount for a new business - especially when you're not having to spend hours creating content for it!

So what makes LinkedIn such a great platform for sales? Simply, LinkedIn is the ultimate relationship building platform. It might not always be as simple to use, but if you are someone who is looking to network professionally and build relationships that come to fruition sooner, then it's super simple to use.

LinkedIn has the benefit of letting you curate your contacts - and choose who you want to connect with based on certain demographics; job title, companies worked for, interests etc. In a similar way to Facebook, LinkedIn also allows you to create communities (although the functionality is very different!) and provides a more professional networking experience. The biggest benefit of using LinkedIn vs any other social media platform, is that it's the only professional platform and the demographic on LinkedIn is a much more professional one, and therefore the prospects using the platform already want to use the network for business related activities. This can speed up decision making times and buying schedules.

Given that LinkedIn provides it's own publishing platform for articles, plus a live video option, it's quickly pushing forward in the social media race. If you want to dominate LinkedIn, you need to be a clear content creator who's prepared to schedule regular posts/ videos/ articles. You are also going to need to be an 'engager'… someone who actively enjoys building relationships and putting in the groundwork of engaging with other people, recommending them and sending cold invitations.

Technology is moving incredibly fast - and as such, we're seeing new social media platforms pop up regularly. Over the last few years, we've seen platforms come and go - or just lose their Midas touch. Facebook, Instagram and LinkedIn (in my opinion) are going to remain the simplest platforms for online business owners to monetise and the easiest to make new connections with. However, if you're looking for great PR opportunities, make sure that you keep Twitter on your radar (and that you regularly search #JournoRequests to try and spot new feature opportunities!)

The biggest caveat to all of this is that you can pick any platform that you want. But it's important that you;

A. Choose based on the way that you like to interact and based on the place your audience is most likely to spend their time.
B. Master one platform before you choose another. It really will make you money so much quicker if you dominate one platform.
C. Understand the best uses of your time - and experiment to find the platform that gives you the best ROI.

My own social media posting strategy currently looks like this;

Facebook:

- Use my free community to provide regular live trainings (1 x per week.) plus daily written content/ engagement time.
- Use my business page to promote automated content; each time I release a blog/ podcast episode, it's uploaded to my business page. I also use my business page to promote any events/ summits that I'm part of as well as paid advertising.
- Personal profile; mainly used for pictures of my dog - and the occasional client celebration / business win.
- Call to action/ sales content; 4 x per week.

Instagram:

- Use LinkTree to promote multiple call to action links.
- Post automated content 3 x per week; podcast episodes and blogs.
- Post regular 'behind the scenes' content - usually twice per week.
- Call to action/ sales post at least once per week.

LinkedIn:

- Regular posts; once per day, Monday - Friday.
- Publishing articles once per month.
- Commenting/ engaging once per day (15 min time slot.)

It might seem like a lot - but in all transparency, I spend roughly 1-2 hours per day on social media in total - but generate a lot of revenue from those channels. Remember, it's not about the amount of time that you spend on the platform, it's about the quality of the content that you put out, the message it sends to your audience and the regularity of your sales / promotional content.

Exercise: Choose the social media platform that you are committing to. Create your own social media plan. Focus on mastering one platform at a time - and figuring out how much free value you'll be giving each week, how many times you'll be showing the 'behind the scenes' and how often you'll be offering the sale.

Netiquette; How to sell in Facebook Groups Without Being Gross

As Facebook is my primary social platform, I'm going to focus the general examples in this section around selling in Facebook communities without being a sleaze. However, remember that you can apply these simple tips to other communities/ forums that you are running or participate in. Just because the tool changes, it doesn't mean that the strategy needs to be 100%

different. Apply the principles and you'll hit the nail on the head each time!

Generally speaking, when we start looking at monetising our message in the online space, we're directed to setting up a Facebook Group immediately or joining multiple groups in the hope of finding clients. It's something that most coaches will tell you (whatever industry you're in) is the easiest method to attract and convert your prospects.

Unfortunately the industry is shifting - and it means that the strategies that worked when Facebook Groups were relatively new, aren't necessarily working in the same way anymore. For example; three years ago, the most popular way to land clients from Facebook Groups, was to pick five groups and post 'value' in each 3-5 times per day. Ideally, you'd also pick a group that allowed promotion and create regular 'YES' ladders (social media posts with the call to action; 'Comment YES below!') and would be able to get regular opt-ins / clients.

However, as time has gone on (and group owners have got more savvy,) it's become more common to see extensive rules in groups including; "No self promotion', 'No pitching', 'No YES / Like Ladders' and other rules that make it more challenging to network successfully. Despite these changes however, there are still ways of using Facebook Groups (both your own and others!) to gain clients consistently, without behaving like a slimeball.

Let’s start with how you can sell in these groups by building relationships. In the online space we preach relationship based marketing and I absolutely stand behind that. I am one of these people that uses this phrase even though it's starting to become overused. I still stand behind the fact that relationship based marketing and relationship based sales is absolutely key for your long-term success. Ultimately people buy from people. We don't buy from the sexy branding, the great logo or the jazzy YouTube cover photo.

Having said that, in terms of becoming somebody that people want to buy from, it means you have to show up as somebody that people actually can enjoy engaging with, that they like, that they trust, that they know, and who they feel adds value to their life on a daily basis. So when you are showing up in other people's Facebook groups, or in your own, the first thing that you've got to really be thinking about is “Am I showing up as somebody that I would want to hang out with? Am I showing up as a person that I would trust, that I would say has integrity? That I would say is the expert in my field? Are you operating from a place of service - or chasing cash?

To be successful, we need to focus on adding genuine value first.

Now that doesn't mean just adding value in your area of expertise, because let's face it, we've all seen the thinly veiled promotional posts that talk at us. The, "I'm a marketing expert and I just want to give you these three top tips about marketing… even though this particular group is about weight loss." Showing up and giving value, means giving relevant value to the audience involved. If you're not able to demonstrate that you've taken the time to research the community and its purpose, it's unlikely that you're going to build effective relationships quickly… and fairly likely that the group owner will haul you over the coals for thinly veiled promotion! So what does real value look like?

- Showing up and sharing tips/ tricks or techniques.
- Supporting other people; answering questions, sharing resources (not your own)
- Recommending other people regularly.
- Sharing valuable free resources that don't compete with the expertise of the group owner. Videos from industry influencers, useful blog content, industry resources etc.

Some of these may feel like they're actually going to lose you business - but it's really not the case. Ultimately, if you are someone who recommends others regularly, you become seen as somebody who likes to connect people.

And if you're a connector, it proves that you are somebody who actually takes pride in building your own network, and who values true connection.

When you focus on being a great participant/ community member and add genuine value, you become somebody that other people want to spend time with. It flags you as being somebody that acts with integrity, who is genuinely focused on the core theme of social media, which is to be social. Communicate with others, connect, and engage.

The second thing that you want to be looking at in terms of adding value is thinking about the kinds of people that you're connecting with in the group. Now, in any community there are going to be three different types of people; prospective buyers, peers/ colleagues and the leader. They all have different roles to play in your business - and your revenue goals.

1. Prospective Buyers.

Prospective buyers are the people that you want to buy from you. In order to move them into your sales cycle, you need to be showing up, adding value and moving them into your own community. They need to see you as the expert in your field - and know clearly how you can help them.

2. Peers/ Colleagues/ Competitors.

I prefer to think of my competitors as 'colleagues' or 'collaborators'. In any industry, you're always going to have some competition - and it can be really useful to spend your energy collaborating with your competitors, rather than worrying about what sales tactics they're using. Spend time networking with your competitors so that they recognise you as an expert. You'll find that if you do this, you'll increase the amount of referrals that you receive. Your competitors can't take every client - and you'll find that they also have niche areas of specialism and that they don't want to cater to every element that you cover. Building a good relationship with your competitors ensures a good pipeline of referrals for both clients and exposure opportunities.

3. Group Leader.

The leader of the group is the person who has created the community. They are usually an influencer who may or may not have more experience/ more established business than you. They may also be a person who is providing a congruent service to you.

It's really important to establish yourself as a good participant with the leader of the community. Think about it, the leader of that community has done something incredible. They have brought a pool of your ideal clients together; whether it's focused on the area that you're focusing on or something that's congruent, and they've managed to keep them there, keep them engaged and monetise the community. Cultivating a relationship with the group leader is key to your long-term sales success within the community. No leader wants to feel like they have a community member who is simply using their community to 'harvest' clients - so it's really important that you build the right kind of relationship with the group leader in order to get more clients without feeling sleazy!

Now, in order to network effectively with that leader you want to be showing up as a good participant. Respecting their rules is basic etiquette. So if they say 'No Pitching' don't pitch. And don't make thinly veiled pitches… because they're worse!

As a group leader myself, I know that I regularly refer my best community members. I shout them out regularly in my own community - and I'll refer them in other communities if I see a relevant opportunity - even if they aren't a paying client! We all reward loyalty - and if you're an engaged and supportive participant, you'll find that the group leader wants to help you in return. Other ideas to network with the group leader without feeling gross are; reporting spam posts and helping to keep the community ‘clean’, ask their opinions on relevant topics (and value the response that you get!) start interesting discussions and spend time helping to support other members. If you do these things and establish yourself as somebody who is going to be collaborative and who is there for connections, the group leader will refer you. They will start tagging you in the group as somebody who has an area of expertise. They'll want to get to know you and they will make you one of the influencers or the influential people in their community. That's huge for you, because it’s the best kind of free advertising; a warm referral from a respected source.

Remember, your network equals your net worth. The people that you know, the networks that you build directly contribute to your cash flow. That's why networking correctly in these communities is so important.

Now you might be thinking, "Yeah, but Jess tell me about pitching now because you're talking about sales, and you're talking about selling in groups, but you haven't talked about pitching yet." I hear you. Pitching is important - especially when it comes to groups where pitching your own services is frowned upon!

In the last chapter, we looked at the 80/20 rule - and this is hugely important when it comes to networking appropriately in Facebook communities. This obviously only applies to groups where you can pitch or sell things. 80% of the time you should be showing up, sharing value. You should be referring people, networking, and be having interesting discussions. Then 20% of the time you should be completely transparent about selling your amazing product/ service or showing people why they should download your latest opt-in.

When it comes to pitching in groups, I prefer open and transparent pitches. If you've been putting the work in to make the community a more valuable place - and they offer the opportunity to promote yourself - then go for it! Be transparent and honest about why people should buy from you. They'll already know, like and trust you ... and they'll have complete confidence in buying from you.

The upside to transparent promotion is also that your confidence in your own product/ service, shows your prospective clients that the transformations are going to be possible for them. When it comes to sales, confidence in your product / service is supremely important - so if you're selling in a half hearted or apologetic way, the audience will assume that you lack confidence in your product/ service... and they won't buy.

Now this strategy will work in communities that allow pitching... but what if a Group Leader doesn't allow promotion? Is it really worth networking in the group? And will you ever get clients from it? YES!

Just because you're not allowed to promote your business, it doesn't mean that a smart relationship builder can't make sales. You'll just need to consider (and implement) two extra steps!

1. Is this group relevant to what you do and are your target market in there?

One of the biggest issues I see with people who aren't able to monetise a Facebook Group strategy is that they're spending their time and energy contributing to groups that don't contain their ideal client. For example; if you're a health and fitness professional and you're spending all of your time in relationship based groups, it's unlikely that you're going to pick up many (if any) clients. Think about it from a consumer perspective; when we are searching for something specific, we're only looking to take in certain information. Information about the product/ service that we're looking for and potentially, products or services that are congruent. People have joined specific communities to engage with the leader (and what they are selling) and already have a relationship with them. If you join a community where you are selling something that is congruent, but not directly competitive to the leader, you'll find you get a lot of referrals... if you adhere to the networking strategy.

2. No thinly veiled pitching.

If you're looking to network a no-promo community and gain clients, it's really important that you operate with integrity. That means; no memes with your website address plastered along the bottom. No links back to your blog/ freebie/ latest video. No lengthy posts that say things like. 'I'm a sales coach so today I'm giving you my three top sales tips... because I'm a sales ninja!' No asking super sneaky 'market research' questions that are secretly leading into your latest offer e.g 'I'm about to launch a [insert product/ service] and I'd love to know if you think [insert element] would be a great bonus for the course/ what you'd pay/ whether anyone thinks it would be valuable'. Thinly veiled promotions will end up getting you removed from the community and ruin all of your hard work. When we pitch in a sly way, it makes our audience think that you are either insecure/ under-confident or that you have no idea how to build and monetise your own tribe. And that's not a good marketing strategy. Instead, create your own 'Facebook Group

Funnel'. Make it easy for people to find and buy from you.

Good ways of doing this include; showing up in the group regularly and adding value - and making sure that your personal profile leads prospective buyers to your sales calls/ products. You can do this by; updating your cover photo to direct people to your own Facebook community or opt-in. Changing your bio/ adding links in to your own business page or lead magnets. These things are super simple but ensure that all of your engagement and hard work isn't wasted in non-promotional communities.

Remember, you're using this organic marketing method to help you attract new clients. It's the first step in your simple sales funnel and is there to help you identify potential ideal clients and bring them into your own community in order to convert them into raving fans and clients. It's really important that you don't just spam a whole host of groups - but that you are consistent with your efforts for 6-8 weeks in order to see results and potential ROI.

Exercise: Identify 3 groups that you are going to network in. Why those groups? Are they congruent to your offering? Create a content plan that helps you appeal to your prospective buyers/ peers and the group leader.

CHAPTER 4: WHY AREN'T MY AUDIENCE BUYING?

Why the F aren't they buying?

Have you ever had that moment of realisation that you're putting a lot more work into your prospects business than they are?

Perhaps you're an online entrepreneur. You've been taught that in order to be successful, get famous and #MakeAllTheMoney that you need to set up a free Facebook community. And then spend all of your time and energy giving free stuff to people who never implement it...

Maybe you're a 'Bricks and Mortar' business owner. You've had it up to *here* with giving out free mouse mats, free samples and branded stress balls... especially when you know that those mouse mats are secretly saving commercial organisations thousands in buying their own replacements.

(I wonder if the mouse mat business is really that lucrative?!)

Or perhaps you're a salesperson working for someone else. You're making ALL the calls. You're doing all of the follow up. And still, you've got clients avoiding the cash conversation - and taking it more seriously than Pablo Escobar took the DEA for the first ten years of building his empire.

The thing is, that sometimes people don't want to buy things. I know - revolutionary.

There is however, a big difference between someone not being in the market for your product or service at the moment - and them constantly consuming your free content… then running for the hills when you pitch to them! So if you're currently plagued by freeple, then read on. Because we're about to retrain you and your audience so that you can make more money - and they can get the results that they actually want.

In fact, the most common reasons that people don't buy are that;

1. They don't know, like or trust you / your product or service enough to get them the results that they want.
2. They don't trust themselves to take the action required to get the results.

Self belief is a huge element of the sale; both for the buyer and the seller. When it comes to the reasons your audience aren't buying, we need to take those reasons into account, alongside the ways in which we are training them to purchase.

In the online space, it can be easy to think that every other marketer is doing a better job of convincing their audience that they have the one power that they need to cure their health/ relationship / business. The reality is that every salesperson is trying to demonstrate the same thing; that they are a credible expert - and that their audience really can achieve their desired result using their product or service.

A few months before writing this chapter, my lovely client Hannah came onto my Smart Leaders Sell podcast and asked this absolute doozy of a question;

"My question would be, if you're just starting out and you're starting your business, how do you make sure that you build a community of people who are trained to buy from you? They're trained from the outset, and that's what happens. And the second follow up part to that question is if you got yourself into that situation, where you have community already, you have trained themselves not to buy from you, or are trained not to buy from you, how do you turn it around?"

And honestly, that question formulates the basis of this entire chapter.

You see, when we start in business (especially online business) we're taught to give away the farm for free. Every expert and guru (myself included!) is telling people to 'give their gold' to their potential customers for free. Because if their first impression of you is of a sub-standard, two page opt-in that is basically just a thinly disguised sales pitch, you'll find that you get tons of unsubscribes immediately.

So why are the gurus telling you to give your best stuff for free? And how can you do that in a way that still trains your audience to buy?

Firstly, we need to look at what is happening when we give our best stuff for free. If it's the first touchpoint that a prospective client has with you, it's quite likely that they'll be wowed - and want to get more of you and your content. Which is great news!

But what if we then move that person to the next stage in our funnel? Across to an email list or a free community where we're constantly bombarding them with amazing free content?

Well that's where it starts to get difficult.

Now it's not to say that you shouldn't give away incredible content for free. I do it regularly and am often told that people buy from me because my free content is so good that they feel that my paid content must be amazing. The one big difference between the way that I deliver my free content and the way that new or inexperienced salespeople deliver theirs is…

I don't let my audience suffer from 'Baby Bird Syndrome' I believe that there are two reasons that your audience don't buy from you.

The first reason that people don't buy is because they're consuming constantly. And they don't understand the difference between consuming and investing. When you consume free information, let's be honest, you don't really give it the attention that it deserves, and you don't actually prioritise it as something to implement, because you're like, "Oh, well, it's free"

Now we all do this. I have an inbox with literally hundreds of unread opt-ins and emails that I fully intended to act on… and didn't. And it's not because I'm a heinous human being who's super lazy. It's just that I wasn't invested in those free things. They might have been excellent… but I didn't have any skin in the game. So I didn't prioritise them, use them or implement any of the information.

With the rise in free communities and the focus on providing constant free value in all of them, what we're actually doing is overwhelming our audiences with tons of information. Imagine being in a dark room, surrounded by projectors. Let's say that there are thirty projectors in the room and each one is playing a different channel. It would turn into a loud mish-mash of colours and noises… but no singular channel would be able to create a lasting impression. Now imagine that you've paid for a cinema ticket. You go into the auditorium, sit in your comfortable well placed seat and relax to watch the film. And if anyone dares talk, sneeze or cough? You're the king / queen of the silent 'Death Stare' to shut them up.

Because you’re invested. You care about the experience.

The second reason is that people don't train their audiences to buy. We're so obsessed with being seen to give value all the time, but we take value as being quantity rather than quality. Now it doesn't mean that you produce endless content and that some of it is low quality.

But it does mean that we are constantly teaching our audience to be like baby birds. And that's what I call, Baby Bird Syndrome. The reality is that we're always turning up in our Facebook groups, or emailing our lists and dropping information into their mouths. We’re effectively taking the mama birds position and assuming that our babies are always hungry - and that it’s always our job to keep them fed with information worms.

The problem is, eventually the mama bird pushes the babies out of the nest and they learn to fly. What tends to happen in the free communities that we build is that we spend all of our time giving for free because we want to be liked and respected as experts in our field… and so when we eventually push them out of the nest and sell to them, we hear crickets. They show their distaste by not buying, not responding and not engaging with any sales based content… and as community leaders, we naturally freak out. And we end up swinging the barometer and going straight back to giving them more stuff for free so that they'll like us again!

After all, you've likely spent months growing the community and encouraging people to engage. But let's put the business hat back on, what is the use in having a large and engaged community if they never hit the buy button? Now this isn't entirely your fault. And believe it or not, (no matter how frustrated you are at your audience members) it's not their fault either. After all, they know you, like you and support you… people aren't inherently selfish tossers that want to screw up your business plan by not paying you.

But people also need to be trained. And your audience needs to be trained early - and learn that sales is a perfectly normal part of their experience. We have to start normalising selling, and help your community understand that free value is great, and absolutely if you action it and you implement it, you can get results. However, that very much depends on the kind of person that you are and whether or not you're self-motivated enough to actually take the information and use and implement it, and whether you honestly value it enough to go and do that.

And we need to demonstrate consistently that if they are the person, like me, who will just end up with never-ending free content clogging their inbox, but they don't take any action on them… then they're the person who needs accountability, feedback and to hire YOU to help them. We need to make it normal and acceptable for them to want and buy the programme. And as coaches, consultants or anyone in a service based industry, we need to normalise the way that we have this discussion.

"Yes, you can use my free content. Yes, if you are this kind of person, and you action it and implement it, it can get you where you need to be. If you are not that kind of person, or you want results quicker, easier, you want to learn from the mistakes that I made so that you don't have to do that, then you need to purchase this paid option".

It really is that simple. And you need to be doing it early, not waiting six months after you've given a ton of value and a ton of webinars. And then you sell and your whole community leaves, because they're freaking out that you want them to pay you for things.

Remember, the more free content that you put in front of people, the more they will consume. And the reality is that the more they're consuming, the less they're implementing. So what we really need to be doing with our sales process is giving value (free) for sure. But then we need to be nurturing people in a way that says, "Here is what you can go away and do on your own. Here is the level at which you can action this content, you can go away, you can implement it, and get results, without falling into a trap, feeling like you've been shortchanged or feeling like you needed more. This is that information. But for the next level, this is what you need. And it is paid content".

We need to be a lot less afraid to actually just say some things. And again, it comes down to setting boundaries. Some things are not free. I can't give one person an entire sales strategy for free, because it wouldn't be fair on the clients that are paying me to be invested in the progression of their businesses.

I think that sometimes, we're so worried about the way that we're perceived. We worry about whether or not we're giving 'enough'. We worry that we need to give away six months of free content before we can 'justify' selling to our audience. In fact the question that I get most often around selling to communities is 'How long do I have to wait or give before I sell to them?

And the answer is, for every free offer you're putting out there, you should be putting a paid offer out there too. You should be selling every single day in your business, whether it's sending out an email to your email list, offering discovery calls, whether it's going to Facebook group and offering a paid program. It doesn't matter what it is, every single day, to some part of your community, you should be offering the next stage in a relationship with you, and leading to that paid service.

So when it comes to analysing why our prospects aren't buying - and how we can train them better, the guidelines are;

- You absolutely should give away great content to attract ideal clients.
- You should nurture your community in a way that normalises the sales process and helps them understand that your free content does lead to being offered paid content. And that that's okay - not a reason for any community destruction.
- Stop giving them ALL the things. Set clear boundaries around what you will give for free and what needs to be paid for.
- Choose your platforms and actions carefully. Make sure that you are interacting and training your audience to feel valued - and value your expertise too.
- Think about what's stopping them; is it a know, like and trust problem, or a self belief issue?
- If you really can't figure out why they're not buying, get some steel ovaries and ask them what's stopping them!

Turning freebie hunters into paying clients

Before I dig into this section, I just want to say that I intensely dislike the phrase 'freebie hunter'. Despite it's popularity, I don't feel that the phrase really fits the intention of most passive audiences. Instead, I refer to those passive people as 'content consumers'. Or, if I'm in mega-strop zone, 'freeple'.

The thing is, that even if they're not buying from you, they may be your most ardent messengers or referral sources. They might be your biggest cheerleaders and supporters. So please, as you go through this chapter, don't just assume that people who aren't making your PayPal account ping, are seeking you out on the internet just to frustrate you and make your life a misery… However, in the instance that you've spent too much time training your audience not to buy… read on and re-jig your strategy and results!

Now let's say that your audience has already been trained not to buy from you. They show up, they consume all of your content and they watch all of your livestreams/ webinars/ YouTube videos. But every time you make an offer, they have an excuse, objection or just ghost you so that they don't have to invest.

Once you've started down that route of give, give, give, the reality is that it's actually a simple problem to fix. But you have to be prepared that some people might not appreciate you for it! Instead of give, give, giving, you publicly say to your community, *"I'm going to rein that in, because I realise that actually, it's really irresponsible of me to give you tons and tons of content that you can consume, but not implement."*

Now some people will love that. They'll immediately understand your boundaries and be really happy that they're not forced to jump on the fifty pieces of content that you're putting out each day.

You can even say that, "I'm going to give you one or two actionable trainings a week, And then the rest of the time, I expect you to be implementing this stuff."

Some people will hate it. They'll accuse you of not giving enough value. They'll blame you for the failures that they're experiencing, and they'll expect you to go back to your normal routine of giving them everything you have for free. Stick with the change - I promise you that it's worth it.

Because dear reader (I still don't know your name!) please don't think that it's just you who has trained your audience not to buy - and then had to retrain them. I did it too - and I've been in sales for years. I trained my audience not to buy. I trained my audience to only accept value. I trained my audience that I would show up in my free community, every single day of the week, and I would give them this incredible free content.

What happened, though, was that it made it very difficult for them to succeed. In fact, they'd be spending so much time consuming my content, that they had no time at all to actually implement anything so, far from my dream of helping people, I was actually keeping them stuck.

Whereas when I turned around and said, "Hey, actually I have got this wrong, I will give you one thing that you can consume," and then you go away and implement it. And if you need something else I'll step up, but you have to commit to the process. And that may mean that you have to pay me." My audience stepped up. They took responsibility for their own sales goals and they went out and made them happen; some with my help and some, just by using my free content and other resources that they had access to.

When we look at turning our content consumers into clients, we have to remember that we cannot force them to buy. And we also have to remember that in joining our free communities, at no point have they signed a contract to say that they are going to buy every product or service that we release forever. In fact, you shouldn't care whether they're buying from you or somebody else.

The thing that you should be focusing on is whether or not, they are actively investing; time, energy or money in themselves, their health/ wealth/ business etc. Now ideally, we also want them to be spending their money with us - but if they don't, and instead, they show up in your community as someone who takes action. Who is a do-er, not just a thinker. Then we still need to value them. Because they'll inadvertently be changing your community and showing them that investing in themselves is key. Your focus needs to be on growing a community of action takers who know when to step up to the purchase plate.

Now this also comes down to you and how you communicate the value of your products or services - and how you communicate the value of them investing in their own growth/ development. Here's an excerpt from the speech that I gave my community when I realised that I'd trained them into only wanting the results - and not wanting to do all of the work required to achieve them.

"The point is, you have to invest in you. You are the primary person in your business, you are the person who is responsible for making the business successful, and keeping it successful, and making sure that it helps impact the world, and pay other people, and all of that good stuff. So if you refuse to invest in your business in any way, money, time, energy, please don't expect other

people to invest theirs in you. If you refuse to spend money oh your business, other people will not spend money on yours.

If you refuse to spend time and energy growing your business, delivering to your clients, giving value, showing up, doing all of the required steps. People will not do that for you. Now you can call it energy, you can call it weird, you can call it whatever you want. But I always say, it's like a mirror in sales, and that is what it is. If you aren't prepared to invest in yourself, if you aren't prepared to step up and say, "Hey, I'm running this business, I'm taking it really seriously," or, "I want to learn about self development, and I actually want to make sure that I make the commitment, that I don't just run away and kind of do whatever I want." Then paying makes it easier.

Actually investing in something will make it a lot easier for you to go through with the hard work. Because when you are paying for something, you show up. I hate fitness. I really, really, really hate fitness. I've hired a personal trainer. I've spent however much, I think it's 250 pounds a month on a personal trainer. And honestly, I've been to every session.

But I went because I was committed, because I had committed financially to making myself the fittest possible version of myself, within a specific time frame. If you want to learn about personal development, or sales, or marketing, or business building, yes you can do it on your own. Yes, you can do it with free content.

But, do not then be surprised when your audience do the same, because what are you telling them? What are you showing them? You're never saying, "Oh, I've invested in this mentor, I've invested in this course, I've invested in this software," or whatever it is that's going to take me and my growth to the next level, so why would they?

We learn from the behaviours around us. We learn from the people that we are closest to, and that we associate with. All of my friends who are my business besties, are people that invest in themselves consistently. They're not out there buying every course on the market. And they're not necessarily the people who spend the most on it. But, they are investing in themselves consistently and they're investing in the right opportunities for them and their business.

So when you're thinking about saying YES to that paid offer, you need to start thinking less in terms of expense and more along the lines of this being an investment into your future. And what that will do is have a direct impact on the money that comes into the business, the impact that we're able to make on more people as a result, the list kind of goes on."

Do you see how that is a different way of communicating the value that investing in themselves can have? Instead of me rocking up and whinging;

"You guys never buy from me. You just don't get that if you don't spend money with me that you'll never

be successful. I want you to stop consuming all of my free content and actually buy my products/ services."

When you're looking to convert your content consumers into clients, you've got to give them a solid reason for wanting to change. Think about areas like;

1. How is not making any investments in themselves keeping them stuck?
2. What is their end goal? And how will investing in themselves help them achieve the goal quicker?
3. What are their biggest fears around investing in themselves? And how can you reassure them?
4. What are you prepared to give them for free? And how far will it get them?

My top tip however, when it comes to turning content consumers into clients is looking at YOU. What are you doing each day to get the sale? To inspire them to buy?

People take it really personally when their community don't immediately jump up and buy from them. But the reality that we really need to look at is, are we selling it? Are we actually talking about it every day? Are we on the newsfeed? Are we talking about it, being really proud of it, talking about transformation that we can give people? Asking people questions as to why they're not buying it, which can be terrifying, but massively useful. Only then can we say that we tried, because putting up one Facebook post and apologetically selling to them, isn’t really selling at all.

And if you are somebody who's thinking, “But when do I sell to my audience?" Every day. Put an up-sell into your email sequence. If you're in your Facebook group, you should be making offers to your Facebook group once or twice a week. The same offer. You don't have to offer a different offer every time, but you should be putting these things out there. You should be offering discovery calls, asking people to get on the phone with you, and conducting proactive marketing campaigns.

People think these things are sleazy. The actual activities themselves are not. The way you do it can be - if you don’t use the correct sales style for your buyers. But ultimately, it's a learning curve. If you don't ever do it, you'll never know how it could have worked out. And you are probably losing out on many, many sales, because actually, there will be people in your audience that do want to buy, but you're just not offering them anything. They’re not mind-readers; they need you to show them what to buy and how to make the purchase.

So before you brand your audience ‘useless’ or say that they ‘never’ buy, just take a step back and ask yourself two questions;

- Am I asking them to buy regularly and consistently?
- How am I training them to behave?

Exercise: Create your own 'content consumers to converted clients' manifesto now. You can record a video, send it in an email or write a Facebook post... but let your audience know that times are a'changing and that they need to get onboard with your new approach.

CHAPTER 5: HOW TO HAVE A SUCCESSFUL LAUNCH

The power of planning.

As my mum would say; fail to plan, plan to fail. When it comes to sales, it's absolutely integral to have a plan. Back in my corporate days, we would focus on a 90 day time period to give new sales strategies time to gain traction and generate results. Since starting my own business, I've found that working in 100 day chunks gives me (and my clients) better opportunities to build new sales habits and test / tweak new sales strategies.

In the online space, planning is especially key to your success. Technology and platforms can change so quickly that it's important to have a solid sales plan in place, that can be replicated across different platforms. To have a successful sales plan, we need to consider a few things;

- What are your revenue goals?
- How much warm traffic do you currently have? (Social media following/ email list etc)
- Price of your offer.
- Planned timelines.
- Any expected content creation/ client delivery or on boarding?

- Key performance indicators; what do you need to do to guarantee an ROI?

Later in this chapter, we'll be mapping out a full launch together so that you always have a four week launch plan to fall back on. Before we get cracking, let's take a look at the easiest ways to plan for success.

1. Know your numbers.

Sales is a numbers game. In order to improve your sales process (and results) you need to know where you're starting from. Get a list of your current revenue generating activities and the results. Conversions that I tend to care about are; percentage of sales calls closed (25% is the average for most people.) Revenue goals… in order to know how many products/ services we need to sell, we have to know how much money we want to make. Buy rate; take a look at the current percentage of your audience who convert from prospect to purchaser. How many people typically convert from your email list/ Facebook community/ other social channels? If one stands out, you can put the majority of your focus there!

2. Be clear on the desired outcomes.

When you're planning for success during a launch or any kind of sales campaign, you have to know your key outcomes, along with the desired outcome that your ideal client is expecting when they make the purchase. Your key outcomes may involve; number of people enrolling, number of booked sales calls, brand awareness and visibility. The desired outcome of your audience is going to be more focused around the problem that they're currently experiencing - and the transformation that they're looking for. For example; they might want to make 10K in 6 weeks, or lose 20 pounds in 3 months. Get super clear about the one big outcome that they're looking for and that will help form all of the content that you'll need to make sure that your launch goes well!

3. Time Blocking.

What time do you have to make sure that this goes to plan? What times in your diary are you blocking off to ensure that you're successful? Try and chunk your time so that you're not constantly context switching; keep to the same tasks for solid blocks of time to ensure that you're not trying to multi-task and wasting energy!

Sales planning really is that simple. With a great plan, an awesome offer and a well thought out launch, it's easy to hit your goals.

Offers: Where is your profit coming from?

In order to make it even easier to hit our revenue / client goals, we have to map out the best offer to hit the goal - and to get the best results for our clients.

The equation that I like to use for this (because hey, #NumbersNerd!) is;

Premium Offer + Warm Traffic = Easy Launch

To generate as much revenue as possible in the quickest/ easiest way, whilst getting the best results for our clients, we have to look at creating offers that are high touch and high ticket. Before you get ants in your pants, high touch/ high ticket doesn't necessarily mean working 1:1 with clients.

Check out some high ticket/ high touch offers:

- Masterminds: If you enjoy working with groups of people and curating interesting conversations and networking opportunities, you could look at running a high level mastermind. These typically do have some kind of curriculum so that you can ensure that people stay on track and are usually anywhere from 3-12 months long.
- Done For You Services: If you're a web designer/ copywriter/ VA/ Ads Manager or similar, then Done For You services are really popular and command premium price points. Think about packages that you can create - or better still, team up with someone in a congruent industry (like a copywriter with a web designer) and work on large joint projects!
- Hybrid Group Coaching Programmes: If you like working with groups, but want a

premium feel, you may want to turn your group programme into a hybrid experience. Adding in some 1:1 calls / Voxer support or email access can really help you dial up the price point and the results that your clients experience.

- Intensive Experiences: People love to learn new things/ get things done quickly. If you can offer a 'speedy' experience, people are more likely to pay premium prices. You're significantly shortening their learning time and giving them the same amount of skills which allows them to have extra implementation time and get results quicker. If you're working on a Done For You basis, you can also run 'rush' jobs; setting up funnels in a day, creating websites in a weekend etc.
- Retreats/ High End Events: Retreats or high end events make great premium offers. They allow the client to be immersed in a different environment and atmosphere and potentially give them access to other people who can enhance their experience.
- 1:1 Work: Coaching, consulting, done with you/ done for you. In the world of online service based businesses, these are all popular options that command a premium price point.

When we're planning a successful launch, we need to pick the right offer for our audience. That means that we need to create the offer, based on market research from our warmest leads. So who are those warm leads?

Your warm leads are the people who already know, like and trust you. They can come from a variety of sources - but the ones that tend to convert best are;

- Previous clients.
- Social media following.
- Email list.

These are people who've all been actively engaging and who are bought into you and your work. They're far more likely to buy - with far less promotion. We call these 'low hanging fruit' - they're the easy wins and will help you generate early profit during your launch period.

Exercise: Conduct your market research. What are your warmest leads struggling with right now? Create a premium offer based on that insider knowledge.

Mapping out your Launch

Once we have our offer mapped out, it's time to get the launch on the road! Now the thing is that launches take work. It's much easier when you have a clear strategy for success, but be aware during your launch that you WILL get fed up. You'll be tired. You won't have energy. You'll get frustrated with non-buyers.

It's all normal - and it happens during every launch. What you have to remember is that a) launching is a finite time period - and it will eventually come to an end and b) your desired outcome. Keep your why at the forefront of your mind so that you stay motivated!

Let's start creating your successful launch plan - and look at the key activities that you have to consider when you're launching anything. The first thing that we need to do is to set goals. It sounds simple, but most business owners feel worst about their launch when they don't set a goal. Setting a goal can be scary - and it can make us question whether or not, we're able to achieve it. But not setting a goal means that you aren't aware when you hit your target and can actually feel worse during the launch because you don't have anything to aim for or celebrate!

When setting your launch goals, you also need to be thinking about the practical aspects too. It's about the amount of visibility your launch gets and the amount of engagement that you get from your audience. It's even about the amount of unsubscribes that you're getting from a email. (And yes, we want unsubscribes during launch time; they signify people who weren't ready / were never going to buy and are dead weights on our email lists.)

So what areas do we need to consider when we're setting goals for our launches?

- How much money you're making.

- How many clients you're bringing in.

- How many people are unsubscribing from your list?

- What does your engagement look like? Are people sharing your offer/ getting excited about your launch process/ interacting with your nurture activities?

- ROI: Where are you spending time, money and energy - and what are you getting back? For example, a lot of people track their ROI on Facebook ads. We're really good at tracking the ROI of a Facebook ad. Everyone's looking at their earnings per lead, but we need to do this with our organic marketing too. How much time are you spending in your Facebook community - and what is the ROI? What's the ROI from your email list?

- What are your KPI's (Key Performance Indicators)? How many emails will you be sending out to get the maximum return? How many Facebook posts will you be putting out there? How much time will you be spending on Facebook live, or interacting and supporting your audience during this period of time? Those things are good to knows. They're good to know because when we come to the end of the launch, we can look at the ROI, we can look at the conversion, but also they're really good for managing your time and avoiding mid-launch burnout.

Most people assume that the launch starts when we open the cart; when we give people payment links. In actual fact, your launch starts before that, and it usually starts with some kind of prelaunch process. Now that can be many different things. Some people use wait lists, some people use teaser activities, competitions, giveaways. Basically, your prelaunch process should be designed to get people excited and warmed up to the idea of your offer. If you don’t run an effective pre-launch process, you’ll find that you’ll leave money on the table. The job of the launch is to get as many eyes as possible on your offer - and if you don’t run a pre-launch process, you miss out on potential eyeballs moving through your launch funnel.

Remember that your pre-launch process needs to appeal to the type of buyers that you’re targeting; aspirational, emotional or FOMO. One of my favourite pre-launch processes for example, is to run a free challenge for my community. Typically, these challenges work really well to bring my community together as a team. They start to enjoy supporting each other - and I get to support and engage with my community.

It also means that when I push the launch button, people are primed and excited to take the next step - together. Challenges work really well as a FOMO pre-launch process; as your community comes together to support one another, they don't want to be left behind when people start buying through to the next stage (particularly for group programmes.) Challenges make people feel included and help them decide whether a community/ group learning environment is right for them. If however you're selling from an aspirational/ emotional standpoint, you're more likely to have success with a pre-launch process that involves a three part video series.

After the pre-launch stage, we need to look at the launch trigger that you want to choose. Launch triggers are the event that causes the opening of the cart. Things like webinars, video series, competitions, giveaways, those things can all be really good ways to hit that cart open button. Now in terms of what will convert best, you need to think about your preferred style of sales. Do you prefer selling face-to-face; video content/ phone calls/ live webinars? Or are you somebody who likes to have a more removed process? You want to be a little bit more removed from it. You want to have the video series that goes into a sales page with a clear FAQs section.

Regardless of the launch trigger you choose, you want to ensure that it's something that is going to be simple for you to set up and simple for your audience to participate in or consume. This is one of the reasons why webinars are so popular because it's 45 minutes of solid gold information and then a pitch, and ultimately something that is going to convert. And if you're someone who really enjoys engaging live with their community, who loves video content and powerpoint slides, a webinar can be an awesome way to open the cart. The key to converting sales from your launch triggers is to have a really good structure for your process of taking that prospective buyer and turning them into a customer… and that depends on how confident you feel. So if you hate creating powerpoint slides but love pre-recorded video, play to your strengths and launch your cart with a simple video series.

The trick with simple sales (and the reason that simple sales strategies are so effective) is to be time efficient. With simple sales strategies, you don't have to stick to the traditional send an opt in, then a $10 E-book, then a bunch of email sequences, then an upsell and so on. During a launch, you get to pick the tools that you use - and the ones that fit you and your audience.

My best advice during a launch is to pick the ones that fit you the best. What are the things that are going to make you confident, that are going to make you happy? Because let's face it, launching is stressful enough without trying to use a ton of things that you don't understand, trusting technology that you've never used, it's all about confidence.

Once we've opened the cart and hit GO on the launch beginning, we need to focus on follow up activity. Sometimes, even with the best intentions, we have crickets early on during our launch process. For whatever reason, all of our prospects are off looking at other offers. To ensure that they don't end up buying from someone else, you need to focus on are your follow ups.

What we tend to forget is the fact that people actually need to have seven touchpoints from you in order to buy. If you've just put out one webinar or three videos in a video series or one Facebook Live, you actually haven't given them that many touchpoints with you. It might feel like you have, but actually you haven't given them the recommended, amount, and some people do take longer to buy than others. That's going to depend on how well they know you, how well they trust you, and whether or not they like you and the offer that you're putting out there.

Having those extra touchpoints helps, and that's where a lot of people fall down. We don't always do the amount of follow-up activity that we need to during launches.

As entrepreneurs, we often get stuck at this point because there's no real hard and fast statistic on the right amount of follow-up activity or how to do it and again, it's because there is no one way. There's no one way that you can be successful. Different launches have different requirements. Different ideal clients have different requirements, different products, services or programs that you're selling will have different requirements, but when you're looking at your launch, you need to be very aware of the tools that you want to use in relation to the product or service that you want to sell. The way that you sell a $30 meditation recording for example, will be very different to the way that you sell a $3000 silent retreat.

Now follow up activities don't have to be complicated, they can be as simple as social media outreach. Reaching out to people in your Facebook group. If this is one-on-one service that you're opening the doors for and you have particularly engaged social media followers, you might reach out specifically to say; 'Hey Amy, I created this offer. I don't whether you've seen it yet, but I'm not giving you the hard sell, I just thought it might be something you'd want to cast an eye over because it seems it'd be really helpful to you right now.'" Your follow-up activity can be that simple. Depending on whether or not you want to bring automation into the mix, your follow ups can become slightly more complex. One of the launch triggers that I often use is a webinar - and I have automated email sequences that go out for 5-7 days after the webinar ends to help people make the best buying decision for themselves. But because these emails are planned out before the launch, and are going out on an automated basis, it can really help me during the busy periods of the launch when I'm starting to get tired and want to slow down.

Having that element of automation, having that 5-7 day email sequence that takes people through the touchpoints, any initial objections they might be having, any fears they might be having about purchasing, any tips and techniques about how they can best use the program or product to their advantage, talking to their desires, sharing testimonials or case studies, those can really help people make an empowered decision.

When you're thinking about these follow-up activities, don't be afraid to get into people's inboxes. They're on your email list, they're on wait lists, they've signed up for your webinar or your challenge or your Chatbot. They want to hear from you and they want to be given the option to purchase from you. Just be sensible with it, and remember that people also want to be offered choice. They want to be offered the opportunity to remove themselves from your launch list, so you can segment them out, and they also want to be offered the opportunity to unsubscribe. Nobody wants to be stuck with a chatbot that pops up every day with a long message but no choice to unsubscribe. When you do that, you remove the person's right to choice - and you back them into a corner where they don't want to buy or stay in your circle of influence.

Remember, the launch process is about giving your audience the choice to buy - or not to buy. It's not to force them into consuming tons of content that they don't need.

Ways to follow up: proactive email outreach, automated email sequences, Facebook lives/ live videos to your communities. You can also use broadcast emails, chatbots and regular social media posts, as long as you are being consistent.

The penultimate part to launching is urgency. Ultimately, we all have fence-sitters in our communities. Many people struggle to make buying decisions; especially when they're making a big investment. Their nerves kick in, the adrenaline flows and they start to question whether or not it's the right decision. This is where urgency comes into play. Urgency is really important during launches - but only integrity based urgency.

It's really important that you don't use false urgency, it's real reasons that person should buy now.

Common reasons of urgency are; the price is rising or the cart is closing. Removal of bonuses (especially any exclusive bonuses) can also be really good reasons of urgency. Don't discount the power of your message or story though. Don't discount the fact that if you send a fabulous testimonial that demonstrates a huge breakthrough moment or result, that final fence-sitters will jump in there too.

Now remember, these are all just tools - and it's about picking the perfect one for your audience. Look at what kinds of buyers your audience are; are they watching the countdown timer? Are they waiting for an inspirational testimonial or breakthrough moment? Don't discount simple things, because launching in itself does not have to be difficult. You don't have to have complex or lengthy launches, in fact, all of the strategies that we've discussed here can be done in two, four or six weeks, depending on how long you want to have available for promotion.

The success of it will depend on how engaged your audience is, how large your audience is, and ultimately how confident you are with all of these pieces and selling.

The final piece to the launching puzzle is the piece that I call the "Double D's" (and no, I'm not talking about anatomy here!) The double Ds are the bits that people often forget during launch time but that are hugely important.

Debrief and Deliver

After your cart has officially closed and you've got your fence sitters to make a decision and you've made those final sales, now is the time to think about your debrief. This is the time where you need to look at, and analyse, what worked well and what didn't. Go back to your KPIs that you initially set, those key performance indicators. Did you meet them? Did you exceed them? Did you not hit them? As a result, what do your sales look like? What does your brand visibility look like? What kind of engagement did you get?

When we do a thorough debrief, and look at that return of investment, it helps us for those next launches. So if Facebook Lives converted clients really well in this launch, but your email marketing didn't produce any results, you know to spend more time before your next launch engaging with your email list to prepare them - and to get as many people watching your live videos as possible.

Equally, we need to look at unsubscribes/ people leaving your community. Did people feel like there were too many emails? Did they get overwhelmed and leave?

Doing your debrief properly will ensure that you know exactly what to leverage for your next launch - and what to leave behind!

Where to put your debrief: Whiteboard, spreadsheet, standard operating procedures. Keep it somewhere that you're going to be able to find it for the next launch.

The second 'D' stands for delivery. How you deliver the product or service to your customers. This is where you need to have processes in place for on boarding new clients, for content delivery and for general organisation.

Having a great delivery process will reduce your refund requests significantly and will ensure that your customers don't experience any buyers remorse. We want our clients to be happy with their experience and the delivery period is a huge part of that.

Delivery process: Is there any content you need to create? How is your client onboard? What is in place to stop them experiencing any buyers remorse?

Those are the steps to launching. Planning your launching effectively, making sure that you set goals, making sure that you have key performance indicators to stop yourself burning out, and then making sure that you actually run the launch in a way that suits you. You can use any of the tools here for your initial launch activity. You can choose any different method of following up.

You can use any real reasons of urgency, that you want in order to get those final fence-sitters, and you can use any way of debriefing that you want to. It's all about making sure your customer feels amazing and that you get the results that you want.

Properly planned launches will ensure that you always get the best results!

Exercise: Four Week Launch Process

1. **Set your goals.**
2. **What is your pre-launch activity? How are you going to warm your audience up?**
3. **What is your launch trigger? When will you be announcing that the cart is open?**
4. **Follow Up activities; sell, sell, sell.**
5. **Double D's; Write out your debrief and start delivering your product/ service to your clients.**
6. **Put these steps on the calendar; week 1 should be starting with your goals and promotion of your pre-launch activity. Week 2 needs to be your trigger/ cart open.**

Week 3 should be your follow up activities and week 4 will include your 'Double D's' and ensuring that your customers are onboard.

CHAPTER 6: HOW TO NAIL YOUR SALES CALLS

Nailing the call

So we're heading towards the final piece of the sales puzzle… sales calls. Pesky little buggers. Here you are, fantastic entrepreneur or sales person, with a great product or service. In fact, I'd wager that with enough hard work and tenacity - your product or service could be a multi-six figure idea. But it's just those sales calls that suck.

You know that the average person closes 1 in 4 sales calls. That's right, 25% of sales calls are successful for average Jess/ Joe. But you don't want to be average. You want to be like me. Jessica Lorimer. Sales Call Jedi… seriously.

In the 3.5 years that I've run my business, I've averaged a 99% SUCCESS rate on sales calls. That's right. 99%. Now I'm not a mind ninja, persuasion guru or blackmailer. I'm normal… just like you.

But over the twelve years that I've spent working in some of the toughest sales environments in the world (oh hey there recruitment!) I've nailed a super simple three step sales call system that, when implemented, is possibly the most dangerously successful sales generation tool in the world.

This sales call strategy is the result of twelve years hard work, hundreds of thousands of 'fuck off and never call me agains', practicing in the mirror, testing every day... In short, it's my own personal sales call bible. And if you use it, practice it and make it your own?

You can't fail.

Are sales calls dead?

Now before we get into the system itself, we need to look at whether or not we really need sales calls and if they still play a part in closing deals.

Back when I was working in my corporate job, one of my favourite mentors was forever shouting at those of us who stuck our heads in our emails all the time.

'Stop fucking tapping and start talking' was heard regularly in our office. And although I'd occasionally startle myself out of sleep, thinking that he was yelling at me, it really was one of the best pieces of advice that I've ever been given.

(Also working in sales, takes brass balls/ steel ovaries and eardrums like rhino hide. And coffee.) So in a digital age, where we can avoid real life human contact for at least a week without a problem, why are sales calls still the most effective way to close a deal?

1. Emails can be ignored. Who else has an inbox with a few *thousand* unread emails? We don't have to answer emails or respond to urgent communication until we're ready… which means that your potential client / prospect can take their own sweet time in answering your urgent plea for them to sign that contract/ pay the bill/ start working with you - and there's nothing that you can do about it.

2. Text can often be misconstrued or taken in the wrong manner. Now this could only be me… but I'm a Brit. Apart from the insane love of tea and London buses (seriously!) I also have a pretty dry sense of humour. Unfortunately my sarcastic wit doesn't always come across in the manner that it's intended in emails. If you struggle to articulate using the written word, it might be causing you to lose clients.

3. We trust people that we speak to. Think about it. Humans judge each other in less than five seconds. Within that time, we make judgements about that person's integrity, character and whether or not we like them. It's actually much easier to demonstrate credibility and establish that you are trustworthy during a telephone / video conversation or a face to face meeting.

Would you buy an Aston Martin in an email? No? Didn't think so. If you're selling premium products or services, be aware that people want to know you, like you and trust you and your product or service before they buy. That means that they're going to have questions, potentially need reassurance and you'll need to ensure that they don't walk away with buyers remorse. That's incredibly difficult to do without real conversation.

In short, sales calls are still very much alive and well. And they really are the best way of selling premium products and services. The good news is, that using the sales call system in this chapter means that you'll give yourself the best possible opportunities to close those sales, and will ultimately start to enjoy selling on the telephone.

Sales call structure

Running the perfect sales call is an art. It takes patience, practice and confidence - but I promise you that following the structure laid out here, that you'll be able to achieve much higher conversions and much easier sales calls than you've ever experienced.

The reason for that is, that sales calls need to be run as sales calls. Now I've been an online service based business owner for the last few years and I can tell you, that in the online space, it's common to market sales calls as something slightly different. So if you're a coach, consultant, healer or any other kind of service based business owner who markets yourself online, you might see a number of your peers or competitors calling their sales calls;

- Breakthrough Sessions
- Assessments
- Clarity Calls
- Complimentary Service Calls.

But I promise you that regardless of what they're called, the intent is still the same. To sell their service to their prospective client. However, renaming those sessions without being clear on what is really going to be achieved, has ended up creating some cynicism in the market.

Instead of being eager to 'hop onto a free call', buyers are becoming much more savvy. They're ignoring those free calls because they fear the 'bait and switch' method… Which basically means somebody positioning the call as 'free' and then giving little/ no value and going in for the hard sell at the end.

Sadly, it's being used all the time in the online (and offline) space and often means that your prospective buyers are wary even before they actually get on the call with you.

So when the market is training buyers to be wary, cynical and avoid contact with salespeople (YOU!) what can you do to buck the trend and still book (and convert!) more calls than your competitors?

Simple.

Be more transparent than your competitors.

Call a spade a spade.

And ultimately, use your sales call promotion to remove fear from the process and increase exclusivity and excitement.

Promoting your sales call

Promoting your sales calls effectively is really important to ensure that you a) get the right type of lead/ prospect arrive onto the call and b) so that you're not forced into the 'giving free advice and making no money' rabbit hole.

I call this process, pre-qualification and it comes from my days in the corporate world. You see, in business, time really is money. So we don't want to be spending valuable sales time on people who have no intention of buying - or worse, no intention of implementing any advice that they walk away with.

In order to combat this, we have to promote sales calls really carefully, and start pre-qualifying those leads coming onto our calls. Now there are two ways of doing this;

Firstly, when you're advertising these calls, get really specific, and I don't mean, "I've got five spaces that just opened up in my calendar and I'd love to offer them to people who want to experience some kind of transformation" Because honestly, it sounds super sleazy and it's been done so many times before. Actually the best way to book those discovery calls in with people that you want to talk to, ideal clients, is to actually be specific, tell people who you want to talk to. That might look like putting out a post that says, "Hey, I'm opening my calendar to talk to people who are…"

And then talk about the characteristics they embody; are they ambitious, are they driven, are they integrity based, are they getting results for their clients but not seeing it reflected in their PayPal accounts. The key thing here is to talk about the specific elements so that the prospect can easily self identify and know that they're the ideal person for this free call.

Then you need to talk about the transformation they want to achieve, My personal pet peeve is when I see people who market with, "Oh I've got these free assessments or I've got these free coaching calls" No - it's not a free coaching call, it is a call where you are going to assess if they are the right client or the right prospective buyer for you, and that doesn't come by opening up your calendar to all and sundry.

You have to get specific about what kind of transformation these people actually really want and know whether you are talking to the woman who wants to lose 10 lbs in 10 days, or if you're talking to the person who really wants to increase their profit margin by $1,000 a day. You need to be highlighting these areas when you're asking for people to come on these calls and the more specific you can get, the more detail and information you can give them about the transformation you're going to provide, the more you're pre-qualifying with ease.

Now this comes with the caveat that these calls are NOT free coaching sessions. I don't believe that free coaching benefits anyone, for the simple facts that a) "People who pay, pay attention" (Russell Brunson, Expert Secrets) People who take free information very rarely do anything with it - or worse, give it a half hearted attempt. And when, inevitably, that half-assed attempt doesn't work, they look for someone to blame. (Yes - that usually falls on you as the person who gave the free advice!) and b) Giving free advice is irresponsible.

Think about it. It's taken you hundreds of thousands of hours to develop your skills. You've had to troubleshoot through a variety of obstacles and have the skills to make links between new issues and problems that you've previously experienced. Someone who isn't an expert (your prospect!) doesn't have this knowledge. And therefore, giving them free advice when you don't have a contract with them or when you don't have the full background required, means that you could inadvertently do them more harm than good… despite your best intentions.

So when you're promoting these calls, be very clear on the boundaries and at no point, should you offer them as 'free advice' or 'free coaching' sessions. Instead, follow my lead and give them a name (I call mine, Supersize Your Sales Strategy Sessions) and market them with the transformation/ result or experience that the person will achieve even if they don't make a purchase.

For example;

This week, I'm opening five spots in my calendar to talk to female entrepreneurs who are currently generating less than 10K per month in revenue, and offering a FREE Supersize Your Sales Strategy Session. This session will help you to; Understand the top reasons that you're not currently generating more than 10K per month in your business, give you a clear and simple action plan to improve those elements and help you move forward with your goal to make 11K + per month from this point forward. Comment below with 'I'M READY TO ROCK MY SALES PROCESS' below and I'll send you a link to book your spot!

Can you see how this type of social media post appeals to a specific individual undergoing a specific problem? It talks directly to the ideal prospect (a female entrepreneur making less than 10K per month) and gives them specific transformation points that the call will help them achieve even if they don't purchase anything.

You might be thinking, "Hang on a second here Jess, you've just told me NOT to coach anyone for free... how are they supposed to get these big results?!" Don't worry - the rest of the structure is going to help you set that out. For now, just focus on promoting the calls and booking more of them!

The specificity of this promotion means that the female entrepreneur who is earning more than 10K per month automatically self identifies and disqualifies herself from booking one of the free calls.

Once we've got our audience to self identify whether or not they're the right fit for the call, we need to ensure that we've got enough information to handle the sales call with them... which brings me to pre-qualification step two!

Exercise: Write out your first promotional / marketing post or email to promote your sales calls.

Pre-Qualification Questionnaire

I have a pre-qualification questionnaire and honestly it is one of the best things I've ever put into my business, for many, reasons, but mainly because when people fill it out, I know that they are super committed to a) coming to the call, being open, transparent and committed to actually making some changes on the call and b) that they've gone through another pre qualifying determination process that is going to help me identify early if this is somebody that's an ideal client for me/ someone who potentially I can help. Or whether this is someone who I may need to refer to a colleague, client or other resource.

In order to work effectively, your pre-qualification questionnaire has to contain the basic information "What's the best contact number for you" "What's your email address" but then you need to focus on subject specific questions that are designed to help you gather as much information as possible about this particular prospect so that you can assess some levels of suitability before you even arrive on the call.

After the basics, comes the juicy stuff! And these questions are important, regardless of what you're selling. Good questions on a pre-qualifying questionnaire will give you the ability to determine what product/ service this prospect is potentially going to need, how urgent their desire for a solution is - along with a whole host of other useful information for objection handling and closing the sale!

Firstly, you need to have a think about what you want to know about your potential client. In order for me to work with someone, I need to know what business they're currently in and what their sales goals are vs what their current monthly revenue generation is.

Think about your business. What do you need to know about your prospective client's goals or current lifestyle? For most service based entrepreneurs, it'll be similar in that you'll want to know what they're currently doing in their business/ life/ health/ wealth/ relationship and what their goals are. For product based business owners, you may want to have a think about questions that address what they need in order to make their life easier/ running their business easier/ cleaning the house easier.

Then you need to pop my secret weapons into the questionnaire; the Red Flag questions. These are the questions that can give you early warnings about whether or not this person is going to be someone that you want to work with. Or whether or not, they're operating from a position of authority/ immediate decision making or urgency.

These are the questions that are designed not to catch people out, because we don't ever want our prospects to feel like we're trying to 'get' them, but ultimately to help us identify, whether or not this person is going to be an ideal client, whether or not they're ready to invest and whether or not they're seriously committed to getting the results they say that they want.

These questions can come in all different shapes and sizes but I want to share a couple of mine with you so that you can integrate them into your own sales process and also so you can start thinking about brainstorming some ideas for these Red Flag questions in your questionnaire. Ones that would be really useful at pre-qualifying people and weeding them out or giving you some red flags that could be identified early and dealt with in that sales call.

So here are a couple of my absolute favourite Red Flag questions; have a think about how you can tailor them to work in your particular industry.

1. "What have you already tried when it comes to your sales process and why did it or didn't it work out?"

This question is huge when it comes to pre-qualifying people in that questionnaire. One of the major reasons is that it helps me identify how self aware my prospective client is. How self aware are they about the things that they've tried and whether or not they really went all out on the things that they tried or whether they held back a little bit and just did the bits that they wanted to.

It also helps me understand what kind of person they are. So for example, if somebody says, "I had 10 coaches and I never got any results because all of my coaches were awful and they never helped me make any decisions."

This would send my spidey-senses into tingle mode because we've all had one bad coach or mentor. Unfortunately it does happen and there are some coaches and mentors out there who haven't always got their clients best interests at heart.

Ultimately though if a client has hired 10 people and write on your questionnaire that none of those people were able to help them, it brings up some warning lights... Is this person really coachable? Do they take full personal responsibility for their actions? Do they take really take action on advice? There are always going to be a few unicorns who truly have the worst luck when it comes to picking service providers - but this question is a great one for weeding out those who are looking for miracle fixes or someone to blame!

The second Red Flag question that I have is multiple choice question and it's about being ready to invest financially in your business at this time. I'm someone who likes to make fast (and correct!) decisions so I appreciate transparency. This means that my second Red Flag question helps the person identify whether they're genuinely looking for assistance / to be coached by me - but also whether or not, they're really ready to jump onto sales calls and make changes to their business.

The question that I ask is;

- Are you financially ready to invest in yourself and your business at this time?

I then give them multiple choice answers;

- Yes I'm financially ready and able to invest in myself and my business.
- I have access to funds that could be used to invest in myself and my business.
- I don't want to invest in myself or my business at this time.

For me, that means saying to somebody, hey, right now are you able to invest in your business securely?

Important Note: (yes… it's important enough that it requires bold text!)

The most important thing to remember about these Red Flag questions is that we do not use these to automatically judge our prospective clients for the answers that they choose -

particularly when it comes to answering questions about finances.

The thing is, that someone else's finances are simply none of your business. What they spend their money on is none of your business. What they choose to find or not find the money for is none of your business.

What *is* your business, is ensuring that regardless of the answer that they choose, you still go ahead with the call. It can be all too tempting to look at someone who chooses the 'I don't have the funds' answer and assume that the call will be a waste of your time.

Honestly? If that's your mentality, you're not going to last long in this game.

You see, the average customer doesn't just buy once. They have a lifetime customer value that is way more than just one sale. So if we make assumptions or cancel these calls, we're giving the middle finger to someone who may be a loyal follower, or a great source of referrals. They might be responsible for sending over your last three customers. So regardless of the choice they make on the questionnaire, it's your responsibility to run the call - and handle it appropriately. And believe me, there is a fantastic way of handling that particular issue without running through an entire call or giving away free advice which we'll be discussing in the next section.

The important thing to remember is that these red flags, particularly around investment questions, can signal how someone feels about being pitched to. It can demonstrate whether or not they're ready to commit to change. But that can all change in their call with you. So make sure that you're open minded and ready to look at what is really going on for your prospect.

Exercise: Create your Pre-Qualification Questionnaire and pop it into your booking system.

Setting the agenda

So we've done the hard part; we've pre-qualified our leads… and now we head into the easy bit. Selling. Okay, you might be thinking "No Jess, the difficult bit is just starting" and I hear you, really I do. But stay with me for a second… If you walk into an Aston Martin dealership for a test drive, do you expect that the salesperson has to do a lot of work?

Honestly?

Of course they don't. The reason is simple. If you walk into an Aston Martin dealership for a test drive, you've already pre-qualified yourself in a number of categories.

1. You're someone who is seriously contemplating driving an Aston Martin and having one as your next car.

2. You have the financial resources available to justify test driving the car (or feel that you will soon have the funds.) People will often disqualify themselves on price alone, so if you've walked into that dealership, you've got, or will have, the cash to pay for the car should it meet your requirements.

3. You need physical reassurance that this is your car and are doing the final checks; will the baby seat fit in, can you actually drive it etc.

It's actually probably easier to sell an Aston Martin than it is to sell a middle of the range Vauxhall. Because someone who's walking into an Aston Martin dealership for a test drive is seriously considering that purchase… whereas someone walking into a Vauxhall dealership has had less pre-qualifying stages to go through. They can still consider other mid-range cars… and therefore, the salesperson has a lot more convincing/ justification to do.

(PS. If you're thinking at this point, premium selling sounds really simple… it is. It's a lot of work when it comes to targeting and branding… but the actual sales process? Super simple and tends to bring quicker decision makers to the fore.)

This is what makes pre-qualification so powerful in our sales process. When we put boundaries in place and make our prospects work to get onto the call they become more committed. They actually show up for the call, and are actually committed to attending, and being open and coachable throughout that process. But the second thing we need to do, we need to actually structure that call for success.

We've all been there. We have all been on those sales calls where the prospective buyer has a huge personality and they come onto the call and dominate the entire thing. You end up feeling awkward and uncomfortable because instead of discussing their business/ life/ wealth/ health/ relationship etc… you've ended up talking about their grandma's birthday, the vet bill for their cat and their son/daughters grades. And instead of moving confidently into a pitch, you're an hour in and wondering how the hell to get off the phone.

We've all had them, we've all been there and it's because the call is lacking in structure and boundaries. Humans actually love structure. One of my clients, Emma, is called the #BoundaryQueen and specialises in helping business leaders and executives set the correct boundaries in their lives and businesses. And as she always says; boundaries make people feel safe. They set the tone. They let everyone know in a simple and easy way, where they stand and how to behave. In short, if you're currently running sales calls without setting a structure, you're leaving yourself and your prospect in sales limbo - and ensuring that an awkward, long conversation that is unlikely lead to sales - is ahead.

So what does this really mean for your sales calls?

It means that you go into the call knowing exactly what you want to do during that call and what your prospect is going to get out of that call and experience too.

It means that we need to openly set an agenda at the beginning of the call so that both you and your prospect can stay on track and keep the call productive and beneficial. It's a really simple tool that people forget about, but that actually really helps you if that client goes off track or if there are things that you need to cover during the course of the call.

So you start by setting the agenda. I find that keeping it super simple helps me get into 'sales' mode and puts my prospective client at ease… they know that there aren't going to be any 'surprises'. Here's the agenda that I typically set;

Hey, FIRSTNAME it's so good to talk to you today, I'm really looking forwards to finding out more about you, about your business, just want to make sure that we maximise our time together today so, first we're going to start talking about this, then we're going to start talking about that, and if it feels right at the end, and only if it feels right, I'm going to share how we work together in future, is that cool?

Setting the agenda this way lets the prospect know what kind of questions you're going to be asking, what kind of participation they're going to be expected to hold up to and also gets rid of that elephant in the room; pitching to them.

We're telling them that we're only going to pitch to them with integrity. So they feel reassured that you're not just a money grabber - but instead, someone who's going to sell ethically and appropriately depending on their needs.

In setting out this clear structure, it ensures that if somehow, you end up talking about grandma Vera's birthday cake, you've got an easy way of bringing them back on track; 'I'm so glad that your grandma had a great birthday - but it feels like we've gone off on a slight tangent here. Let's get back to..."

In the last section, I mentioned that this was also a great time to raise any red flags that you noticed on the prospects questionnaire. After you set the agenda, simply start with;

"I want to start with an answer that I saw in your questionnaire… I noticed that you answered that you don't have any access to funds to grow your business / invest in your health/ hire a PR person right now. Could you let me know what your current situation looks like - and your expectations for the solutions that you'd like to see from me so that we can make sure we're all clear on what's going on"

Phrasing it this way has a couple of benefits. It doesn't raise the hackles of the prospect; instead it gives them the option to take some responsibility for their answers and be held accountable to them. It also makes them think about why they chose that particular answer and give you the honest reasons behind it.

Over the last 3.5 years in my business, I've had a lot of people who've ticked the 'lack of funds' box. But actually on raising the question, they've admitted things like;

"I didn't just want to come on a call and be pitched for the whole thing"

"I'm not sure that I'm ready to invest in my sales strategy yet"

"I didn't want to get the 'hard sell' for something I don't need"

As those answers come out, it's your job to either allay their fears - or shut the call down. The only time I shut a call down if is someone refuses to be pitched, even when they know that I'm only going to offer them something if they're the right fit. The reason for me, is that these people are uncoachable and their refusal to be open-minded means that I'd not only have to drag them through the sales process, but also the coaching process as a whole. In those instances, I just say politely; "I hear what you're saying. And in order to ensure that I don't waste your time or mine, I'm going to end this call now. I can only give advice to people that I know are going to be open minded and implement it and I don't feel like that's your current status."

I'm not going to lie, it takes ovaries of steel to say - but it's saved me hours on calls with non-ideal clients that I know I don't want to work with and can't help. If however, someone tells me that they're totally strapped for cash, I'll still go through the call. I'll recommend the solution that I think best suits their situation - and it's their choice if they're able to find the money or not. If they're in hardship, I send them to some of my best free resources or low paid products and recommend that they implement everything and come back to talk to me in 3-6 months.

You'd be surprised how much loyalty that gains. Helping people and genuinely serving them will gain you a prospective client who'll recommend you or refer you even when they can't pay you themselves. And nine times out of ten, they'll come back again too.

Hopefully you're now seeing the power that setting a clear agenda affords you when it comes to your sales calls. Because it's not just about the money. It really is a conversation that helps you interview the clients, and empowers them to make the right buying decision for themselves.

Exercise: Write out your own agenda and pop it on a sticky note somewhere clearly visible.

Discovery phase

After we set the agenda, we move onto the Discovery Phase of the sales call. Now this is the part where you get to be really nosey and where you get to find out a lot about their business. The reason that for doing this isn't because you're really obsessed with not talking on these calls but simply because knowledge is power.

The more information you have about somebody, about the transformation that they're looking for, or the way that they want to move their business/ health/ life, or whichever area that you're covering forward, the easier it is to avoid objections.

We're going to talk about handling objections, but if you use this structure, you won't get that many of them. So using the Discovery Phase properly really helps us to set ourselves up for success and makes sure that you gain as much information as possible at the beginning of that call to help you avoid those objections later on.

The questions that we ask throughout this phase are super simple, but designed to get you the important knowledge that you'll need to handle objections, summarise and sell later on in the call. As one of my former mentors says, 'You have two ears and one mouth for a reason'. The whole purpose of this call and using this structure is that it's your prospect who should be doing most of the talking, so that you can provide a supportive sales environment and pick up on buying cues and choose the right product or service for them.

During this phase, we ask the basic questions;

- What kind of business do you have?
- What do you want it to look like in three months time?
- What kind of transformation are you looking for?
- What are your timelines for achieving that goal?
- In an ideal world if I could give you a magic wish from a genie, what would you like your life, your health, your relationship, your business to look like after 12 months?

- If we came back to this conversation in 12 months time and I asked you what had changed, what would you want to see?

These are all great questions that you can use in that discovery phase to understand exactly where your ideal client is right now and what they're looking to achieve. If you listen and actually hear what they're saying, rather than thinking about how much money you can get out of them later, you'll find that you end up with smooth running sales calls that convert with ease and you'll be able to use those transformation points to help sell them into the offering the programme, product, or service that you have that genuinely can help them.

Key Note: Make sure that you take copious notes during this phase - and that you record your sales calls to help you figure out how to tweak your calls to make your conversion rates even higher!

Pre-objection handling

The Pre-Objection Handling Phase is where you can probe your prospective clients with questions that establish what is stopping them from hitting their goal. The questions that you ask in this section will be responsible for ensuring that a) you are better equipped to handle any objections and b) gain a better understanding of the prospect and what their real problems are.

This phase will give prospective buyers a breakthrough with regards to their current situation. For example, we all know that when we want to lose weight, we need to eat less and move more. The reality however, when you ask your clients why they feel like they don't follow that advice, is that they start to think objectively about their situation and will share the real truth about the reasons that they've not been actioning the advice until now.

A lot of people come to me and they explain that they're really, really struggling to close sales calls but when we ask during this phase how many sales calls they actually have a month, they say two or three. Actually their problem is lead generation, or community building. If they could turn around and do anything differently, what would they do? Where do they perceive their problems to be in the future.

(And if my personal trainer is reading this, I now know that I can't use any more time-management excuses. I've well and truly milked the 'But I'm writing a book so I can't possibly lift that weight/ run that extra mile')

The questions that you'll typically ask during this stage include questions like;

- "So I hear that your goal is to make X amount of money per month, what do you feel has been stopping you so far?" This is the point at which that person will raise all of their fears. They'll talk about perhaps things that you feel or you know are irrelevant when it comes to that problem being solved and they'll also raise any problems they have that are valid.
- "What have you already tried? What worked / didn't work?"
- "If you could turn back time and do anything differently, what would you do?"
- "What do you perceive your future problems to be when it comes to [achieving your goal]?"

If you're a coach/ consultant, you can also ask them questions about their ability to take action/ take constructive feedback or be coachable. Ultimately, if you're going to be coaching somebody through a problem, you need them to be able to be open and receive feedback rather than getting defensive. So this is your opportunity to find out any potential obstacles that have stopped them in the past and whether or not you'll be able to help motivate and keep them accountable to move past that obstacle this time.

The other thing you can do in this stage is you can handle objections proactively here. So for example, before you move on to any kind of sales or summary stage, you can say,

"Okay based on where we are now, would you see anything stopping you moving forward if there was a proven plan in place to help you get from point A to point B right now?"

This gives the prospect the opportunity to ask any questions that they have or to talk about anything that they feel they might be concerned about in that instance. It might be that they're already starting to worry about the price tag and so you can legitimately address any concerns they do have right at this point. That being said, if you get past this point and you think, "Okay that person is not an ideal client because they don't exhibit the characteristics that I'm looking for or they don't have a problem I can solve" Then the next phase in the call is going to be different for you.

If however, you get to the end of this stage and feel like you've gathered enough information and are confident that you're ready to move forward to the pitch… read on!

Exercise: Make a note of the Pre-Objection Handling questions that you want to use in your sales calls.

The Pitch

It's important that throughout the sales call, your prospective client feels like you're really listening and understanding their needs. It's really important that before you make the pitch, you give them a brief summary so that they know you've listened and are about to give them a solution, based on the information that you've gathered.

Now, if your prospect isn't an ideal client and you've decided that you don't want to work with them or aren't the right fit to help them, you need to use your summary to demonstrate that you've listened - and to shut the call down and send them elsewhere. I find that keeping it simple makes it easier and saying something like;

"Okay, to my knowledge, this is what I understand your problem to be, this is the transformation I understand that you want to get, I'm not the person who is going to be able to help you get there and instead I'd recommend" And then either you can recommend a colleague or refer them to a free resource and tell them to check back in with you in three months or so when you feel like they'll have had time to implement and be ready to move forward with your services. Prospects really love it when you're honest with them - and having the integrity to be able to tell people that this may not be the right time for them to spend money on your services because they need to do more work / get to the right level to get the best results with you, guarantees you a lifelong fan. They'll also have a network of peers with similar problems and be referring them all to 'the salesperson with integrity'.

If however, you have gone through this process and the person is the right fit; they exhibit the characteristics that your ideal clients do, they have a problem that you can solve and you know that they are an ideal client just waiting for you to take them to the next level, then now is your time to summarise back to them,

"Okay, I understand that your problem [insert problem] and the transformation you want is [insert desired goal] I know that I have something that can help you, would you like me to outline that for you?"

This is important because again, you're getting their permission to sell to them. After you have the 'a-ok' it's your job to sell your product/ programme or service. A couple of top tips here are to focus on benefits, rather than features. One of my clients, Judy, says that facts tell, stories sell. But in the sales world, I tweak that slightly to become, facts tell but transformation sells.

Ultimately, your prospect cares about the outcome or transformation that they're going to achieve - not the amount of videos that they're going to have to watch/ PDF downloads that they'll need to print or calls per week. Those things are important to making sure that they get the results - but your pitch really needs to focus on the transformation that they want to achieve and the benefits of working with you to get there.

One thing that I'm forever telling my private clients is; "Sell them what they want, give them what they need' In short, no-one wants to be told that in order to lose ten pounds in two weeks that they're going to need to show up to the gym at 4am, eat only chicken breasts and fish eyes and run twenty miles per day with a ten kilo weight bag. Now that might be exactly what they need to do (in which case, I'm never going to push for that drastic weight-loss!) but they don't need to hear that during the pitch. They need to hear about their ultimate desired outcome and your confidence that you can help them get there.

So for example; "I know that over a 12 week period we would be working on [insert points] to make sure that your ultimate goal of hitting those 10K months, every single month would become your new reality. In order to do that we'd be meeting every week and we'd be setting clear action plans to help you generate immediate revenue, to help you scale your community and to help you automate your business so that you're not working 24/7 in order to hit those huge money goals"

How much better does that sound than, "We're going to meet once a week and we're going to talk for 45 minutes and then I'm going to give you this PDF and then you can have email access so that if you have access you can send them over to me"

It's simple. It's easy and it focuses on the goal that they want to achieve.

Once we've outlined the programme/ product or service that is the best fit, we need to close the deal. So you give your pitch and finish with; "How does that sound?"

In asking them for their opinion, you're giving them another opportunity to raise any potential problems or talk about how great they feel this solution is for them. Bear in mind that if someone gives you feedback, that a good salesperson will always tailor their offer. So if someone asks for more 1:1 time / fewer sessions per week, it's absolutely fine to offer them a slightly different or tailored solution. Tailoring however, does require confidence and practice so that you're not spending thirty minutes trying to work out a new offer and price - and if you're working for someone else, please know your own responsibility and what you're allowed to offer / negotiate to.

So we've got their permission to talk about the offer. We know that they're happy with the solution on offer…we need to talk price. Price is typically the part of the pitch that trips up a salesperson. Let's face it, saying the price can be nerve-wracking. Especially if you're in a position where that sale really matters. Back in the first three months of my business, I remember thinking about every sale and thinking; 'This one could be the difference between me paying the mortgage and being able to go to Tesco or me living on the year old Pot Noodles in my cupboard…"

It's easier said than done, but trying to relax in this situation will help. Stay calm and state your full price - then be silent.

Sales conversation rely a lot on psychology - and the psychology here tells us that the person who speaks first after a period of silence, is the weaker personality. Now that doesn't mean that you or your prospect is boring or easily manipulated, but sales relies on confidence - and a clear demonstration of confidence is the ability to sit in silence whilst your prospect considers the price.

Once you've said the price, don't go off on a tangent. A lot of people have been taught that we get on the phone, we tell them the price then we discount the price, then we try and talk as much as possible in order to make them buy so it kind of ends up sounding a little bit like, "So yeah that's going to be $5,000 and actually there's $1,000 off today but if you buy within the next 10 minutes then I'll give you an extra $250 discount and by the way I'll also sell you my first born child for that too"

Ultimately, our brains do not work at the speed of light and if you throw a ton of options at somebody, their brain gets really confused and confused minds do not make buying decisions. So tell them the price and then be silent, be calm. If they come back to you and they say, "Okay I can't afford that" - great news, you now have two options to help navigate the close.

1. You can take them back to the Pre-Objection Handling Phase by saying something like, "Okay, that's cool. I've been really honest with you throughout this process, so I just want to check in here. Is this really a question about the price or is there something that I haven't covered off that would help you make this decision?" So you're not judging them, you're not asking them to sell their sofa or their car or anything to pay for your services - you're just asking them to be honest with you. This also gives your prospect the ability to tell you if they need more information or ask you for more reassurance about specific aspects of the service.

2. You can also talk to them about the possibility of a different service altogether; "Okay, let's say I had something else that would help you achieve these parts of your transformation that you're looking for but you wouldn't necessarily get as much one on one time. Would you like me to outline that for you because it's more within your budget?" If you use this option, please make sure that you don't try and cram the original service into something lower priced, just to make the sale. Manage the clients expectations accordingly and set clear boundaries. After all, we can't drink champagne on a beer budget - no matter how much we'd like to!

So what happens if they come back with objections?

Objections are simply requests for reassurance. The one that we tend to worry about most often is price - but statistically, the money objection is only real around 2% of the time. That means that the other 98% of objections are really around things like; self belief / confidence, needing to talk to a partner/ spouse or decision maker/ wanting reassurance that the product or service is really the right fit.

If you get any objections, handle them with care - instead of trying to give them the hard sell. The formula that I use is;

- Empathise: Empathise with their objection and let them know that you understand.
- Reassure: Show them how overcoming their objection and buying would be a good idea.
- Educate: What are the consequences if they buy into their objections and don’t purchase? Where will they be in three/ six or twelve months?

When it comes to handling objections and closing the sale, you need to be thinking about how you can make this an open space and an empowered space for that person to make the buying decision? Ultimately, during the sales call you want them to walk away, ideally, buying from you. Most importantly though, you want them to have made a decision. Are they a, "Hell yes, I want to work with you and I'm signing up right now and here are my credit card details”, or are they an, "Actually this offer isn't for me. You've given me some food for thought, and I appreciate it, and I'm going to go off and do whatever it is that I need to do before I come back to you at a later point."

Either is fine, don't be afraid to get a no. No's are good, the more no's you get, the more yes' you are on your way to receiving. Remember that this call is a decision making call. It’s a call where you are in control and able to help them make a decision then and there rather than letting go of the sales process and losing the sale.

There are going to be some instances where people have to go away and talk to their partners about investing, they're going to go away and want to think about it, that's absolutely fine too, but just remember before you get off that call to arrange a follow up; don't be afraid to say, "I'm going to check in with you at [insert time] on [insert date] so that we can make sure that there are no other questions you have and that you're ready to make the best decision for you, okay?" Once you've done that most people will be absolutely happy that you'll follow up with them, they'll feel really good about it and they'll have a decision on the time/ date that you've agreed.

However, if you've run your sales process in the same way that we've laid out here, you'll find that you have far fewer objections… and that the majority of your prospects will be a YES! `When they say yes, make sure that you make the sale easy for them and reduce any potential buyers remorse. This can be as simple as taking their payment details over the phone and letting them book in their first session/ reassuring them of their order or delivery date and making sure that your last words to them are focused around how happy you are that they purchased and how confident you are that they're going to get the results that they want.

Recap: In order to run a successful sales call you need; to pre-qualify your audience and ensure quality leads coming onto your sales calls. To set a clear agenda and follow the structure to collect the best information and support your prospective client throughout the buying process. To be able to handle objections, focusing on empathy, reassurance and education. Remember how it feels to make a big purchase and don't be afraid to provide a safe environment for your prospective client to make the best buying decision for themselves.

CHAPTER 7: FINAL NOTES

Writing this book has been a labour of love. If you've made it through to the end, then you now have the exact tools that you need to help you;

- Identify your own sales style - and use it to convert more prospects into paying customers.
- Choose the best social media sales platform for you - and convert your audience into clients.
- Understand what may be stopping your audience from buying and how to rectify it.
- How to plan and map a successful launch.
- How to nail any sales call.

I completely credit my business success to these five elements. They are simple, they're manual and they're not 'sexy'. But they work. And I promise you that if you've made it this far, and you've completed the exercises, that you are well on your way to becoming the ultimate salesperson. All I ask? That you drop me an email to let me know how you get on!

And if you have questions, feel free to email me; Jessica@JessicaLorimer.com or join The Smart Leaders Sales Society on Facebook. I'd love to see you there!

ABOUT THE AUTHOR

After spending over a decade in corporate sales, Jessica Lorimer decided to quit the 9-5 (read: 70+ hours per week and a strong caffeine addiction) and swap it for an awesome online business, teaching online business owners how to create simple, authentic sales processes that actually work! (read: ditch the scary sales funnels and start building a simple sales process that gets you happy paying clients!)

Jessica launched her business, Smart Leaders Sell, in 2014 and rocketed it to a multi-six figure coaching and consultancy business in less than 3 years. She was ideally placed to share her experience after a corporate career as one of the industry's highest performing sales people, with a stack of company awards to show for her success.

She now teaches her simple *three step sales system* to entrepreneurs who want to learn to sell as individuals with integrity and helps them rapidly skyrocket their sales success and profit margins.

Learn more about Jessica at SmartLeadersSell.com

BONUS RESOURCES

If you're ready to start putting my discovery call magic to work for yourself, I have an unadvertised bonus for you: *Top 10 Ways To Book More Sales Calls.*

Go to Bitly.com/BookMoreSalesTop10 in your favourite web browser and follow the instructions to download your copy for free.

THANK YOU'S

This book would not have been possible without the help of many people. In fact, there are too many of you to name who've given me advice, support and responded to my endless market research requests over the last few years. But a few notable mentions go to;

My Mum. The strongest, most inspirational woman that I've ever met. You raised a firecracker… and I'll forever appreciate you telling me to 'invest in myself - or no-one else will'. That one phrase changed my life, and the lives of so many people in my community.

Sam. You make me happier than I've ever been. I couldn't ever put into words how you make me feel … but luckily there is a song for every occasion! I'll pick one every week and sing it to you. This book wouldn't have been possible without you - and nor would the business. You're my partner in crime, Chief Stationary Officer and the only person who can make me smile when I'm in a strop. Thank you for everything that you do - I really am the luckiest person in the world to have found my perfect person.

To our families. I know that over the last couple of years, I've worked (even at Christmas!) and I really appreciate you all just letting me get on with it and never complaining. Nana Pearl -

you're the best grandma anyone could have and all of your texts make my day. Tracey, John and the cats… thanks for all the board game giggles, furry midnight snuggles and the reminder to always brush my hair! Tony, Tracy and Achilles for festive walks and wine. Oh and Jack… who's going to be responsible for publishing the next one of these books. Remind me to keep it short and give me some funky diagrams.

Jacquie and Jonathan. The smartest people I know with the best taste in food and wine. For the last five years (!) you've both been on hand for classical music concerts, bone jokes and osteopathy treatments. And full credit goes to Jacquie for keeping me sane in the corporate world. Without our prosecco and olive evenings, I may have ended up stabbing myself with a biro. Thank you both for fuelling our weekends with good wine, great food and better company.

My biz bestie Heather. The most talented mindset ninja that I've ever come across. Our daily chats across the pond have kept me sane, made me laugh and have always inspired me to keep moving forward. Your commitment to the bold truth and complete honesty is so refreshing in a world full of crazy marketing and reminds me every day to be a better business owner. And to Damon too for letting me steal his wife's brains each day and who never minds our crazy voice message chats. Thank you both so much.

To my community; my amazing Dotties and clients. I am so proud of you all. Every day, you step up, take more action and inspire me to be a bigger, braver and better version of myself. I wouldn't be able to do it without you (or all of the gifs, memes and regular comedy posts that we share!) I truly value each and every one of you… and without you, this book would not be here.

My incredible team… Beth for keeping my inbox organised and my sanity intact. Scott for producing the best podcast on the planet, Dan for being a wicked mentor and reminding me to always 'keep my shit together' and Amanda for working hard to keep my name in the press. You are all phenomenal and I couldn't have done it without you.

And finally, my amazing tribe. You guys are just the best. And I celebrate every single time one of you makes a sale. Know that regardless of whether you're a podcast listener, group member, lurker or otherwise… I'm rooting for you. And I know that you really can do anything you set your mind to.

Printed in Great Britain
by Amazon

77159974R00099